Theology in the Making

Biography
Contexts
Methods

Edited by
Gesa E. Thiessen & Declan Marmion

VERITAS 2005

First published 2005 by
Veritas Publications
7/8 Lower Abbey Street
Dublin 1
Ireland
Email publications@veritas.ie
Website www.veritas.ie

ISBN 1 85390 945 9

A catalogue record for this book is available from the British Library.

Designed & typeset by Paula Ryan
Printed in the Republic of Ireland by Betaprint, Dublin

Image on front cover shows 'The Conversion of Saint Augustine' by
Fra Angelico reproduced courtesy of the Thomas Henry Museum,
Cherbourg.

Extract from 'April' by Patrick Kavanagh on p. 30 is reproduced
courtesy of the Jonathan Williams Literary Agency.

Extract from 'Emerging' by R.S. Thomas on p. 155 is taken from
Collected Poems 1945–1990 published by Dent, 1993.

*Veritas books are printed on paper made from the wood pulp of managed
forests. For every tree felled, at least one tree is planted, thereby renewing
natural resources.*

Contents

Contributors

Una Agnew Ph.D. read English and Irish at University College, Dublin, in the 1960s. From 1970–1974 she studied Spirituality at Duquesne University, Pittsburgh, USA, and in 1991 completed a Ph.D. on the work of Patrick Kavanagh, under the guidance of the late Professor Augustine Martin. She has taught in Ireland, France and California and has been lecturing in Spirituality at the Milltown Institute of Theology and Philosophy for the past twenty-five years, where she holds the position of Associate Professor. At present she is head of Spirituality at Milltown Institute. She contributed to *Neglected Wells: Spirituality and the Arts* (Four Courts Press, 1997). Her book, *The Mystical Imagination of Patrick Kavanagh: A Buttonhole in Heaven* was published by Columba Press, Dublin, in 1998. She lectures widely on Kavanagh's work and has contributed articles to a variety of journals. She is a member of the congregation of St Louis.

Mary Condren Th.D. gained her doctorate at Harvard University in the area of Religion, Gender and Culture. The author of many articles on liberation and feminist theology published in international journals, her first book *The Serpent and the Goddess: Women, Religion, and Power in Celtic Ireland* was published by Harper Collins in 1989 and by New Island Books in 2002 in Dublin. She has taught at Harvard University; University College, Dublin; Trinity College, Dublin; and at the

Milltown Institute of Theology and Philosophy. She is currently director of the Institute for Feminism and Religion at University College, Dublin.

James Corkery S.T.D. received the B.Soc. Science from University College, Dublin, in 1977, the 'Bakkalaureat in Philosophie' from the Hochschule für Philosophie, Munich, in 1979, the B.D. from Milltown Institute in 1984 and his S.T.L. and S.T.D. from the Catholic University of America in Washington DC in 1986. His S.T.L. thesis focussed on the social dimensions of grace in Leonardo Boff and his S.T.D. thesis on the relationship between human existence and Christian salvation in the theology of Joseph Ratzinger. He has taught systematic theology at Milltown Institute of Theology and Philosophy since 1991, where he is now Associate Professor. He was head of the Department of Systematic Theology and History 2002–2005. His publications include *One City, Two Tiers: A Theological Reflection on Life in a Divided Society* (co-authored, Dublin: Cherry Orchard Faith and Justice Group, 1996), 'Spirituality and Culture' in *The New Dictionary of Christian Spirituality* (SCM, 2005), 'Does Technology Squeeze Out Transcendence – or What?' in *Technology and Transcendence*, (Columba, 2003), 'Unripened Fruits' in *Windows on Social Spirituality* (Columba, 2003), 'Continuing to Think about Faith and Culture...' in *Studies* 92:365 (Spring, 2003), 'One Christ, Many Religions' in *Milltown Studies* (Winter, 1997) and 'The Idea of Europe According to Joseph Ratzinger' (*Milltown Studies*, Spring, 1993). He is a member of the Jesuit Order in Ireland.

John D'Arcy May Dr Theol., Dr Phil. was born in Melbourne, Australia. He received his S.T.L. from the Gregorian University, Rome, in 1969 and his Dr Theol. (Ecumenics) in Münster in 1975. He was wissenschaftlicher Assistent at the Catholic Ecumenical Institute, Faculty of Catholic Theology, University of Münster 1975–1982. He was awarded the Dr Phil. (History of Religions) in Frankfurt in 1983. He worked as Ecumenical Research Officer with the Melanesian Council of Churches, Port Moresby, and as Research Associate at the Melanesian Institute, Goroka, Papua New Guinea, 1983–87. He was Director of the Irish School of Ecumenics, Dublin, 1987–1990 and is now Associate Professor of Interfaith Dialogue at the Irish School of Ecumenics, Trinity College, Dublin. He was Visiting Professor in Fribourg, Switzerland (1982); Frankfurt, Germany (1988); Wollongong, Australia (1994); Tilburg, Netherlands (1996); and Australian Catholic University, Sydney (2001). His publications include *Meaning, Consensus and Dialogue in Buddhist-Christian Communication: A Study in the Construction of Meaning* (Peter Lang, 1984); (ed.) *Living Theology in Melanesia: A Reader* (Goroka: The Melanesian Institute, 1985); *Christus Initiator. Theologie im Pazifik* (Patmos, 1990); (ed.) *Pluralism and the Religions: The Theological and Political Dimensions* (Cassell, 1998); *After Pluralism: Towards an Interreligious Ethic* (LIT Verlag, 2000); and *Transcendence and Violence: The Encounter of Buddhist, Christian and Primal Traditions* (Continuum, 2003).

Donal Dorr D.D. was a lecturer in the 1960s in philosophy in Cork University, Ireland. He then taught theology in various colleges in Ireland and later in Africa. From 1979 to 1983 he held a Research Fellowship in the Theology of Development in Maynooth College, Ireland. He spent many years in founding and staffing training programmes and support networks for community activists in various African countries and in Ireland. He was researcher/resource-person for the Irish Missionary Union and has also served as consultor to the Pontifical Commission on Justice and Peace. He is the author of several books, including *Time for a Change: A Fresh Look at Spirituality, Sexuality, Globalisation, and the Church* (Columba, 2004); *Mission in Today's World* (Columba/Orbis, 2000); *Divine Energy: God Beyond Us, Within Us, Among Us* (Gill and Macmillan/Triumph

Books, 1996); *Option for the Poor: A Hundred Years of Vatican Social Teaching* (Gill and Macmillan/Orbis, 1983, revised and expanded edition 1992); *The Social Justice Agenda: Justice, Ecology, Power and the Church* (Gill and Macmillan/Orbis, 1991); and *Integral Spirituality: Resources for Community, Justice, Peace and the Earth* (Gill and Macmillan/Orbis, 1990). He is an Irish missionary priest.

Seán Fagan Ph.D. has more than forty years' experience teaching, counselling and writing in Europe, America, Africa and Asia. He is the author of *Has Sin Changed?* (Michael Glazier/Gill & Macmillan, 1977) and *Does Morality Change?* (Liturgical Press/Gill & Macmillan, 1997; re-issued by Columba Press in 2003). He is the author of numerous articles on moral theology, spirituality and religious life. He is Emeritus Lecturer in Moral Theology in Milltown Institute were he still teaches in Adult Education programmes. He was Dean of Philosophy at the Institute and lecturer on ethics and moral theology. A Marist priest living in Dublin, he was Secretary General of the congregation in Rome from 1983–1996.

Seán Freyne S.T.D., L.S.S. recently retired from the Chair of Theology at Trinity College, Dublin. He is currently Director of Mediterranean and Near Eastern Studies, a Joint Research Programme between the School of Religions and Theology and the School of Classics. He is a Fellow of Trinity College, a Member of the Royal Irish Academy, a Trustee of the Chester Beatty Library, Dublin, and he is President-elect of the Society for New Testament Studies (SNTS). He also served on the editorial board of the International Journal for Theology, *Continuum*, 1986–2000, and co-edited several numbers of the journal dealing with the Bible. He has been closely associated with the development of Jewish Studies and the Herzog Centre at Trinity College. His research interests and publications cover the broad areas of Second Temple Judaism and Early

Christianity in the context of Greco-Roman antiquity. Specifically, he has concentrated on Galilean society in Hellenistic and Roman times, with a special focus on the interface of archaeological and literary evidence. His published works cover such topics as economic issues in antiquity, the social world of the gospels and Jesus and Paul within the context of Jewish restoration hopes. His most recent publications include *Texts, Contexts and Cultures* (Veritas, 2002) and *Jesus, a Jewish Galilean. A New Reading of the Jesus Story* (T. & T. Clark International/Continuum, 2004).

Michael Paul Gallagher Ph.D. entered religious life after studying literature at universities in Ireland and France. He did further research in literature and theology at Oxford, John Hopkins and Queen's University, Belfast, where he obtained a doctorate in theology. From 1972 to 1990 he lectured in English and American literature at University College, Dublin. From 1990 to 1995 he worked in the Vatican in the Pontifical Council for Dialogue with Non-Believers and the Pontifical Council for Culture. Since 1995 he has been Professor of Fundamental Theology at the Gregorian University, Rome. He has published numerous books of spiritual and pastoral theology. These include *Struggles of Faith* (Columba, 1991); *What Are They Saying about Unbelief?* (Paulist Press, 1995); *Free to Believe: Ten Steps to Faith* (DLT, 1996, revised edition); *Dive Deeper: The Human Poetry of Faith* (DLT, 2001); and *Clashing Symbols: An Introduction to Faith and Culture* (DLT, 2003, revised edition). He is an Irish Jesuit priest.

Werner G. Jeanrond Ph.D. studied theology, German and philosophy at the Universities of Saarbrücken and Regensburg, and received his Ph.D. in theology from the University of Chicago in 1984. He taught theology at Trinity College, Dublin, between 1981 and 1994. Since 1994 he is professor of Systematic Theology at Lund University, Sweden. He has served on many editorial boards, including *Concilium* (1991–2001), the board of the Swedish Research Council and the Nordic Research Council for the Humanities (2001–2003), and is currently editor of *Svensk Teologisk Kvartalskrift*. His main publications, which have been translated into several languages, include *Text and Interpretation as Categories of Theological Thinking* (1988, German original 1986); *Theological Hermeneutics* (1991); *Call and Response* (1995); *Guds närvaro* (1998 and 2005); and *Gudstro* (2001). He is currently working on a theology of love.

Vincent MacNamara D.C.L., D.Phil. has taught at Maynooth College and at Trinity College, Dublin, and currently lectures at Milltown Institute of Theology and Philosophy, Dublin. He has been visiting lecturer at the Gregorian University, Rome. His publications include *Faith and Ethics: Recent Roman Catholicism* (Gill and Macmillan/Georgetown University Press, 1985); *The Truth in Love: Reflections on Christian Morality* (Gill and Macmillan/Michael Glazier, US edition *Love, Law and Christian Life*, 1988); and *New Life for Old: On Desire and Becoming Human* (Columba, 2004).

Enda McDonagh D.D. gained his doctorate from the Pontifical University, Maynooth, and a D.C.L. from the Ludwig-Maximilians Universität, Munich. He is Professor Emeritus of Moral Theology at the Pontifical University, Maynooth, and Chair of the Governing Body of the University of Cork. He is also a member of the International Aids Funding Network Group (AFNG) and Ethical/Theological Advisor to CAFOD, London and to Trócaire, Ireland. He is the author of numerous publications. The most recent include *Vulnerable to the Holy* (Columba, 2004); *The Reality of HIV-Aids*, with Ann Smith (Trócaire/Cafod/Veritas, 2003); and *Religion and Politics in Ireland*, (ed.) with J.P. Mackey (Columba, 2003).

Mary T. Malone Ph.D. studied classical languages and early Christian literature in Dublin, Manchester and Toronto. She completed her doctoral thesis on *Christian Attitudes towards Women in the First Four Centuries: Background and New Directions* in Toronto. She was Associate Professor of Religious Studies at St Jerome's University and the University of Waterloo and Assistant Professor in Church History at St Augustine's Archdiocesan Seminary, Toronto School of Theology. Her publications include *New Parish Ministries* (Novalis, 1982–1983); *Who is My Mother?: Rediscovering the Mother of Jesus* (Wm. C. Brown, 1984); *Women Christian: New Vision* (Wm. C. Brown, 1985); *Step by Step: Handbook for the RCIA* (Wm. C. Brown, 1985, revised 1989); *Women and Christianity*, vol. 1, *The First Thousand Years* (2000); vol. 2, *From 1000 to the Reformation* (2001); vol. 3, *From the Reformation to the Twenty-First Century* (2003, all by Columba/Novalis/Orbis) as well as many articles in journals in Canada, USA, Britain and Ireland.

Declan Marmion S.T.D. studied theology in Passau, Dublin and London. He received his doctorate in theology from the Catholic University of Leuven, Belgium, and is currently Head of the Department of Systematic Theology and History at the Milltown Institute of Philosophy and Theology. His publications include *A Spirituality of Everyday Faith: A Theological Investigation of the Notion of Spirituality* in Karl Rahner, Louvain Theological and Pastoral Monographs (Peeters/Eerdmans, 1998); (ed.) *Christian Identity in a Postmodern Age* (Veritas, 2005) and (ed.) with Mary Hines, *The Cambridge Companion to Karl Rahner* (Cambridge University Press, 2005). Research interests include contemporary trinitarian theology, the relationship between theology and spirituality, and the theology of Karl Rahner.

Geraldine Smyth Ph.D. was Director of the Irish School of Ecumenics (1995–1999) where she is currently Senior Lecturer in Ecumenical Studies and Co-Director of a project on churches and peace-building in Northern Ireland. She was prioress of her Dominican Congregation and consultant with the World Council of Churches. Her writing embraces creation theology, church and politics in Ireland and the theology of ecumenism and peace. Her publications include *A Way of Transformation: A Theological Evaluation of the World Council of Churches Conciliar Process on Justice, Peace and the Integrity of Creation* (Peter Lang, 1995); *The Critical Spirit: Theology at the Crossroads of Faith and Culture,* co-edited with Andrew Pierce (Columba, 2003); and (ed.) *Distance Becomes Communion: a Dominican Symposium on Mission and Hope* (Dominican Publications, 2004).

Gesa E. Thiessen Ph.D. is Reader in Theology at Milltown Institute of Theology and Philosophy and Honorary Research Fellow at the Department of Theology and Religious Studies of the University of Wales (Lampeter). She studied at Tübingen University, at the Irish School of Ecumenics, Trinity College, Dublin, and gained her Ph.D. at Milltown Institute of Theology and Philosophy in 1998. She is the author of *Theology and Modern Irish Art* (Columba, 1999) and *Theological Aesthetics – A Reader* (SCM and Eerdmans, 2004). She has contributed articles to numerous theological journals. Her research interests include theological aesthetics, ecumenism, theology and culture, and mystical theology.

Elochukwu Eugene Uzukwu Ph.D. is Senior Lecturer at Milltown Institute of Theology and Philosophy, Dublin. Formerly he was Rector and Lecturer at the Spiritan International School of Theology, Enugu, in Nigeria. Between 1979 and 2000 he lectured in seminaries and institutes in Congo Brazzaville and Congo Kinshasa, and in

Nigeria. He is Visiting Lecturer at the Institut Catholique de Paris. He is chief editor of the *Bulletin of Ecumenical Theology*, published in Enugu, Nigeria. His publications include *Worship as Body Language: Introduction to Christian Worship: An African Orientation* (Liturgical Press, 1997) and *A Listening Church: Autonomy and Communion in African Churches* (Orbis, 1996). He has also contributed many articles to academic journals. He is a member of the Spiritan Order.

Introduction

Gesa E. Thiessen & Declan Marmion

Over the last few decades biographies and autobiographies have experienced unparalleled interest in the public domain. Bookshops now devote specific sections to this genre. It seems our longing to know how other people live and manage to survive (or not) either in the past or in our fragmented, pluralist, highly individualised society is insatiable. Wonderful biographies, written by eminent scholars, open up the lives of those who have become household names, whether in the arts, the sciences, history or politics. At the other end of the spectrum there are the more popular biographies and autobiographies of sports and film stars, many of which have been ghost-written and sometimes before the person has reached the age of thirty.

The latter scenario fortunately does not come into play in this volume. Our focus is on a selected number of Christian theologians who are Irish or who have worked in Ireland for a considerable period. Theologians are sometimes caricatured as rather quaint creatures who study God and matters religious in an abstract and speculative manner, often at a remove from the concerns of everyday life. We hope this volume will put that myth to rest. In short, we want to explore what are the motivations and convictions that undergird the theologian's vocation. It is rare indeed to come across reflections by theologians on their scholarly development and how this is connected to the vagaries of their biographical journey and vocation. The essays here, however, attempt just this. Each is quite personal in nature. A glance through the contributions of these theologians demonstrates that their life and theological work cannot be separated. In other words, theology is an existential pursuit, arising from the questions and challenges of life, and is to a greater or lesser extent concretely linked to the theologians' life stories, to their personal and societal contexts, influences from the past, the epoch in which they live and their geographical location. The autobiographical reflections collected here therefore testify to a theological life and to a spirituality. Theology is a passion, not just a 'job'; it comprises a vision of Christianity and a way of life.

In recent years, two books were published which have served as a stimulus for our project: *How I Have Changed* (SCM, 1997) edited by Jürgen Moltmann and *Shaping a Theological Mind* (Ashgate, 2002) edited by Darren C. Marks. Each book comprises reflections by leading contemporary European and North American theologians on their life and work in theology. Not only are they a joy to read, but the essays provide seminal insights into their theological and personal interests, views and development. They open up the world of theology not so much from a historical, systematic perspective, as in introductory books to theology, but from that very personal perspective of a life-long commitment to the pursuit of faith seeking understanding that is theology.

Our idea was to do something similar for established theologians from an Irish background or who have worked in Ireland for some time. Thus we have included scholars from Ireland, Australia, Germany and Nigeria, men and women, lay and clerical. All are, as one might say, on the wise side of fifty. Most are in their mid- or maturing careers, while a few are *emeriti*. A glance at their biographical details reveals a wide range of publications, as well as personal familiarity through study and work with the theological situation in Germany, Italy, Britain, France, Sweden, the States, Canada, Africa, Australia and Papua New Guinea. Far from being 'limited' to Ireland, what strikes the reader is the breadth of personal and theological experience which comes to the fore in these pages. In approaching the project, we provided the contributors with a few guiding questions. At the same time we intended that they should feel free to attend to those questions in the way they considered appropriate, while adding their own interests or emphases. Our questions focussed on how they found their way into theology. What attracted them to this discipline? What were the main theological questions that have occupied them through their career? How did their theology change and develop over the years? Further we asked how Ireland had impacted on their engagement in theology and where do they see the relevance of theology in contemporary Ireland. Related to this question is the place of theology within the university today and how they would like to see theology develop at third level in Ireland. And finally, we asked them about their theological hopes and concerns for the future.

These questions have been addressed to a greater or lesser extent by each contributor. However, it is striking that the focus in the majority of the contributions is primarily on their own theological biography, that is, on their history and development as theologians. Moreover, all share a Catholic background. (An invitation to some non-Catholic theologians, including two women, had to be declined due to previous commitments.) While all the contributors are of Catholic background, this does not imply a limitation; instead, it has highlighted some common themes that have affected all the contributors in one way or another.

Most of the contributors belong to the generation of the Second Vatican Council and its aftermath. A wind of change moved through the lecture halls for many who studied theology 35–40 years ago. The high hopes attached to the post-Vatican II period of church renewal carried and inspired those studying at the time. It is not surprising then to note a sense of disappointment and frustration of hopes unfulfilled. It is clear, moreover, that several of the theologians in this volume who have devoted their lives to scholarship and to the academy have suffered for their convictions. While they have been inspired by the injunction 'to give an account of the hope that is in you' (1 Pet 3:15), they have had to put up in some cases with misunderstandings and marginalisation. Thus a career in theology could entail personal struggle and even the prospect of censorship. There is a sense that the renewal inaugurated by Vatican II has been slowly clawed back and that in some quarters of the Catholic Church there is a harking back to a pre-Vatican II state of affairs. There is a further sense that a climate of fear is restricting open dialogue between theologians and the community. The lack of freedom of speech and the strong centralising tendencies in the last two decades have had a bearing on the work of some of the scholars in this volume, as elsewhere. Theologians, especially moral theologians and those working in institutions with an ecclesiastical affiliation, often find themselves looking over their shoulders and reluctant to say what they really believe. The line between heresy and orthodoxy is not always a clear one, however, and many of the outstanding and provocative theological voices of the twentieth century (for example de Lubac, Rahner, Congar, Schillebeeckx, Boff, Dupuis, to name just a few) faced reprimand or censure at some point in their careers.

Several of the theologians here have engaged with difference – intercultural, interreligious and interdenominational – for most of their academic lives. This encounter with otherness, while pursued with intellectual rigour, is at the same time intricately tied up with the personal life-story of the theologian concerned. Thus an abiding commitment to ecumenism can be traced to early family interactions with other Christian denominations (G. Smyth), while the Eurocentric focus of traditional theology spawned an interest in the religious challenges of the Asia-Pacific region and subsequently to dialogue with other religious traditions (J. D'Arcy May).

Another dimension, which is apparent throughout, is theology's ecclesial context as well as its public character. We have already alluded to the sometimes-fraught relationship with the ecclesiastical institution that a number of the contributors have had. Yet each has tried to listen and to take seriously the faith questions and struggles of believers – both past and present. In that way there is a strong sense that theology must relate to life's concerns. While theology as a subject disconnected from the faith questions of believers and the life of the church may be an option to some scholars, theology devoid of an ecclesial context and a responsibility towards the community is not one which features here. There is, in fact, a strong sense of responsibility towards the church, society and beyond. One has only to note the serious engagement with political questions, the environment, with the role of women in Christianity, inculturation and mission etc. that characterise these scholars' work.

Finally, what is impressive is the honesty and integrity in all the contributions, the sense of personal journey, as well as a sense of self-effacement and humour. We would like to express our appreciation to each of the contributors for making this volume of theological biography possible. It is our hope that those who are setting out on their theological studies, as well as those who have already spent many years in this wonderful discipline, may find here some inspiration and encouragement for their own theological journey.

Feast of St Augustine, 28 August 2005

I.

My Way to Spirituality

Una Agnew

A Christian 'as a matter of course'

Reared in a homogeneous Roman Catholic background, in a rural community near the borders of Louth and South Armagh, I was, until well into adulthood, what the Danish philosopher Søren Kierkegaard called, 'a Christian as a matter of course'! I was imbibing Christian values around me in a relatively unthinking way, for the most part, asleep in my facticity. Religion was important in my home; my parents being the local educators in a rural community where people's welfare mattered a lot. Theirs was the generation destined to experience for the first time the new Constitution of Ireland (1937) and restore the country's dignity as a self-determining nation. My father was a devotee of the family rosary, my mother read the Bible instead of fiction during Lent and as children we accused her teasingly of being a Protestant!

The Mythical/Religious Culture of South – East Ulster

Ours was a home dominated by children, storytelling, politics and football. Legends of Sliabh Gullion, St Brigid of Faughart, Ferdia and Cuchulainn of Ardee, the Children of Lir and the Cattle Raid of Cooley: all intertwined themselves in a frequently exasperating web of fact and fiction. This ancient countryside of the Fews[1] was rich in story, rhyme and song with smuggling folk-tales adding extra local colour. My mother supplemented her genius for storytelling with a diet of good books, poems and deep respect for chapel and clergy. School and chapel were inextricably linked in our lives, enclosed as they were in the ancient ring-fort space that formed our playground; a haven of faith and culture! Fairy-lore haunted and stretched the imagination while love of nature was instilled by a multitude of wildlife, a panoramic view of patchwork fields and the ever-varying tints that adorned Sliabh Gullion's brow. The dream of a Gaelic language revival refused to die; its roots injected a sense of God and invisible energies into the names of fields, lone-bushes and rural way of life.

The Nurture of Spiritual and Aesthetic Sensibility

Despite its natural deprivations, boarding school at St Louis Convent, Carrickmacross, provided a nurturing ambience for aesthetic sensibility. Private prayer was fostered in the dimly lit atmosphere of the convent-chapel after evening study. Plainchant song and the rich melodies of choir pieces, musicals and operettas imprinted themselves indelibly in the memory. A love of beauty and culture almost filled the gap left by absence of home and loss of rural landscape. Devotional practices in the shape of May altars, Children of Mary and Legion of Mary cultivated an adolescent desire for God's ministry at this early romantic stage of religious development. In many ways this aesthetic/devotional culture of boarding school was more faith nourishing than the diet of Hart's Christian doctrine, Sheehan's Apologetics and Gospel learned by rote that fulfilled the requirements of a largely stolid and uninteresting Religious Education syllabus. The decision to become a Sister of St Louis at eighteen seemed a natural sequel to boarding school life of the late 1950s. I was guided unconsciously, more by the example of happy religious women around me than by conscious personal conviction of my own. After four years' study at UCD I graduated with a BA and Higher Diploma in Education with a brief to teach Irish and English in the West of Ireland. Then, unexpectedly, I was assigned to a teaching post in France.

From France to the USA

Exposure to French culture came with the Student Movement at its height in Paris, 1968. In the nearby medieval-type village of Juilly where I taught, life was calm and undisturbed. With my senior Baccalaureate students, I was enjoying the French liturgical renewal with the hymns of Lucien Deiss and Jo Akepsimas. Modern religious music stirred French Catholic youth into more active participation in Liturgy. Where the French church was alive, it was exciting. I was enjoying a more self-questioning form of faith than I had left behind in Ireland. It was then timely that a Dutch Spiritan, Dr Adrian van Kaam, Director of the then 'Institute of Man' at Duquesne University Pittsburgh, came to speak to members of my religious institute in Ireland. All were enthused by his interpretation of *The Vowed Life* (1968). His 'three-fold path' emerged from experiential foundations already incipiently present in the human person and even foreshadowed in animal life. This way of life he argued, served the culture in a profound three-fold attitudinal response to persons, events and things; a healing programme of life formation. Van Kaam's revolutionary formulation of the vows at that time was made in response to humanistic arguments, which I had already encountered among my students who viewed the vowed life as unnatural and, frankly, a waste! His conviction that the theological foundations of the vows were rooted in the deepest aspirations of the human self made more sense to me than attempts to force their origins exclusively from biblical sources or even from history.

What is Spirituality?

Van Kaam had been propounding his seminal spirituality theory in terms of 'human existence' that 'gradually differentiates itself and integrates itself according to a project of existence.' My life was experiencing enormous differentiation. Could it find integration? The religious mode of existence, when central, 'can permeate all other modes of being in the world'.[2] This was a programme for life. As a young apostolic religious woman, I was excited by the notion that a 'central religious mode of presence' integrates and renders all other modes holy. I was fortunate to be sent by my religious congregation as a post-graduate student to Pittsburgh to study under the guidance of this intellectually alert and thoroughly modern spiritual master. Van Kaam was then (1970) already engaged in defining spirituality as a science, in terms of its primary and secondary formal objects. He worked tirelessly to explicate a suitable interdisciplinary methodology for spirituality as well as explaining a rationale for so doing. He painstakingly distinguished the discipline of spirituality from theology and explained how the rupture between these two distinct (not separate) sciences had occurred. The writers Jean Leclercq and Louis Bouyer became significant authors, along with his already strong commitment to existential psychology. Van Kaam believed that theology had long enjoyed pride of place as a formative religious discipline; its role now was to inform, not dominate, spirituality. Needed as a complementary discipline was the formational/informational theology to which he has devoted a lifetime's work. The insights of this scholar were and remain a predominant spiritual and intellectual influence in my life.

Adrian van Kaam's Anthropology of the 'Self'

Understanding Van Kaam's anthropology and his definition of spirituality as a science, became perhaps, the greatest personal investment of my life. For me it has stood the test of time. Going beyond a neo-Freudian construct of the self, he devised his own self-theory inclusive of universal religious spirit as well as Christian articulation. He had succeeded in incorporating much of the realism of Freud without losing anything of the spirituality of Aquinas. His understanding of the human self as 'openness to Mystery' was spiritual, existential and psychological. His thinking originated when, as a seminarian, he helped hide people during the underground movement in Holland in 1944–1945. The challenge, at that time, was to help people of various religious traditions and none to be open to life-formation in the light of 'the divine mystery' central to 'human unfolding'. This experience as well as his work at Brandeis University forced him to devise a language that was acceptable to all creeds and none; thus he initially made reference to 'The Holy' and 'the sacred dimension of life' as central to life-formation. Literature and psychology were twin disciplines revealing the meaning of human existence. Human experience was the starting point of both.[3] As his thinking developed in the 1980s, he moved away from the more humanistic phraseology pertaining to self-fulfillment and emergent selfhood and came to speak freely of disclosing 'the Christ-form within us' through 'graced Christian unfolding in daily life'. Dialogue with Abraham Maslow revealed the divergence in these two authors' approaches to transcendence. Although Maslow disagreed with van Kaam, he respected his 'effort to expound a transcendent personality formation centered on the grace of a personal God'.[4] In contrast, Maslow's self-actualising self drew on no such divine intervention. Grace was an unpopular concept at that time.

Van Kaam's courses at Duquesne University (1970–1974) were exciting originals but always grounded in experience. He had no illusions about his emerging science of spirituality. He encouraged his students to become 'masters of suspicion', confront authentic and inauthentic ideals in self and others, unpack personality structures and peal back the layers of human experience to disclose its structure, using a phenomenological methodology. Guarding against mere humanism, he kept his teaching in tune with Catholic doctrine, drawing on the riches of the mystics and masters of spirituality. He ensured that his books always carried an

Imprimatur. His classes over these three years were small (ten to twelve students) which afforded optimum student–teacher contact. Emphasis was placed on reflective journaling as a means of integrating course material and providing a testing ground for thesis work. Needless to say, he experienced considerable resistance on the part of students who believed he was not theological enough. Van Kaam, for his part, did not wish to lessen the importance of theology as a science, but struggled to show how it must *inform*, not *supercede,* its respected partner, spirituality. When, some day in the distant furture, his complete opus is retrospectively assessed, it will be seen that he, in partnership with Dr Susan Muto, was working towards the eventual formulation of a theology of applied formation.[5]

Originality and Spirituality

My research in Duquesne dealt with a topic considered fundamental to the spiritual life. It concerned *Originality and Spirituality: The Art and Discipline of Being Oneself.* Guided by van Kaam's theory I maintained that the foundations of authentic selfhood are rooted in one's biogenetic make-up, historical cultural roots and deepest Origin – God. The methodology used was interdisciplinary and required philosophical, psychological and sociological foundations. Alvin Toffler's bestseller *Future Shock* appeared on second-year book lists and demonstrated forcibly that world trends, in particular the accelerated pace of change affecting people, products, communities and organisations, was beginning to affect the very stability in which the original self could be nurtured. Buffeted by the ever-increasing pace of change and multiplicity of lifestyles, the individual found it difficult to remain true to innate original promptings.

The thesis had to be firmly rooted in human experience – *my* experience![6] Taking my courage in hand, I began to make explicit my lived experience of originality, taking cognisance of those obstacles within me that were blocking original selfhood, as well as what facilitated its ongoing emergence. I had to live the thesis, have it intersubjectively validated at research seminars, as well as study its far-reaching academic implications in the library. William Luijpen and Merleau Ponty gave the lead in how to investigate experience phenomenologically, how to plumb the universal structures of a lived experience and discover its foundational components. Literature was a strength I brought to my research and I was encouraged to use its experiential riches. Once selected, the thesis became a lens through which lectures and reading materials were assimilated. Summers were spent investigating and annotating bibliographies. Duquesne University had been the intellectual home of William Luijpen, Bernard Boelen and Remy Kwant. Mircea Eliade and Rollo May were also resident or visiting lecturers there so that some or all of these names began to appear in students' bibliographies. Van Kaam's interdisciplinary methodology sent us delving into new areas of the human sciences. Biogenetics was essential to originality. Although DNA testing was not yet to the forefront of people's thinking, Van Kaam was insistent that genetics played an essential role in discerning the blueprint of the soul before God.

The Writings of Søren Kierkegaard

It was the philosophy of Kierkegaard which impacted on me most. I was assigned *The Point of View of My Work as an Author*[7] for a project directed by Dr Susan Muto. Schooled in interpretation by Paul Ricoeur, her approach to reading and her method of interpretation began to influence the manner in which I read.[8] I allowed Kierkegaard's words to reach me at the very level of my existence, just as he intended. He was guiding the reader towards his cherished category – the individual – urging me to reflect myself out of the mass-mindedness of 'Christendom':

> Who thou art I know not, where thou art I know not, what thy name is I know not. Yet thou art my hope, my joy, my pride; although unknown thou art an honour to me. (1962, p. 109)

I 'slow' read my way through *The Point of View,* phrase by phrase, confronted by ideas like: 'the crowd is untruth and 'the individual' is the category through which, in a religious respect, this age, all history, the human race as a whole, must pass'. I remembered 'The Pass of Thermopolae' from school and shuddered in the self-recognition that 'only *one* attains the goal'. Kierkegaard's notion of individual selfhood was a 'category of the spirit, of spiritual awakening'. The shift in consciousness was seismic. Having experienced, to date, two major culture changes and a major earthquake along the San Fernando Valley Fault in 1970, Kierkegaard's words had easy access to my psychic and spiritual vulnerability:

> Eternity which arches high o'er and high above the temporal, tranquil as the starry vault at night, and God in heaven who in the bliss of that sublime tranquillity holds in survey, without the least sense of dizziness of such a height, these countless multitudes of men and knows each single individual by name. (1962, pp. 111–112)

His words touched the very quick of my selfhood. Reading Eliot, Hopkins, Thoreau and Dilliard, I was exploring new levels of spirituality in literature. At the same time Evelyn Underhill's classic volume, *Mysticism*, absorbed me by her profound understanding of the mystical journey. As a fellowship of learners and friends in Duquesne, we kept each other grounded through this transforming process, with the help, when needed, of a much trusted Mexican American spiritual guide and psychotherapist, Dr Charles Maes.

To have learned research skills, in a computer-less age, from the combined competences of van Kaam, Dr Susan Muto and Dr Carolyn Gratton, I now see, as one of the great gifts life has offered. I completed the thesis, explored on five different levels, and applied its findings as a formative tool in the final chapter. The proposal for this thesis was published in Adrian van Kaam, *In Search of Spiritual Identity* (1975). Van Kaam was proud of his students' work and thought to publish a Spirituality Series consisting of this pioneering research, but few were free to avail of his invitation. After three years' study leave, religious communities required some immediate return for the valuable study opportunity that had been granted. As a result, many valuable pieces of research completed then are still gathering dust. Few Irish religious women in the late 1970s were writing. Women religious were heroically engaged in pastoral and administrative work in schools, hospitals or on overseas mission. I soon became heavily involved in Renewal work called *Focus for Action,* sponsored by the Conference of Religious of Ireland, and lived for some years from a suitcase! Services as a spiritual counsellor were also in demand, since religious life in Ireland was reeling in a fast-forward movement of modernisation and enculturation. This acceleration cried out for a new spirituality, one to be lived privately 'at home' but not for study in the academy!

You Can't Go Home Again?

What became evident in Ireland in the late 1970s and early 1980s was that spirituality was unknown as an academic subject. It was truly a golden age of theology in the Mater Dei Institute when I accompanied my formation students there from 1974 to 1980 and found there a gifted staff in full academic flight! While I enjoyed sitting in the benches with my students who were in formation, I knew I was neither fish nor flesh. I was not a trained theologian, yet not a neophyte either, my training had been as rigorous as any in the area of spirituality. I was now learning from great theologians, though I could see that theology as a discipline needed further application to life and embodiment in reality. I remember noting in John Macquarrie's *Principles of Theology* (1966) that, although *experience, revelation* and *culture* were named as three of the formative factors in theology, these received nowhere near the same attention as *scripture* and *tradition*, the traditional cornerstones of the discipline. Dermot Lane's enthusiastic lectures on 'the Christ-event', his emphasis on a 'low-ascending theology', his probing insights into Tillich, Pannenberg and Moltmann should have guaranteed my thorough and immediate re-conversion to theology,[9] but having made the shift in Duquesne into the field of experiential knowledge, I could not make the shift backwards. I still believed that theological concepts and critical analysis, however excellently taught, often fail to transform Christian consciousness.

Gradually, I found myself engaged in a bit of everything: pastoral ministry, personal counselling, spiritual direction, retreat, personal formation work; I lost confidence in spirituality as an academic subject. I often wonder, were I a male religious with the same training, would the situation have been different? I was occasionally employable, it seemed, in the area of personal development (how van Kaam would have wept!). Nevertheless, in 1985, Rev Jim McPolin S.J., offered me the Directorship of the one-year Spiritual Studies Programme at the Milltown Institute. This programme consisted, almost exclusively, of theology! I thoroughly enjoyed my involvement with it, my course on *Personal Religious Formation* and the much needed spirituality infrastructure built around the programme. Through my work in Milltown at this time, I met wonderful men and women who have gone on to do great things for church and for theology. They continue to inspire me.

By 1989, it finally dawned on me that spirituality as a discipline had no real place in a theology faculty, although Sandra Schneiders had just published her groundbreaking article 'Spirituality in the Academy' in *Theological Studies* (1989). The problem was not confined to Ireland; it was widespread. This is one reason why, in 1995, the Institute of Formative Spirituality, my *Alma Mater* at Duquesne University, Pittsburgh, closed down and was reborn as a non-profit *Epiphany Association* with its Academy of Formative Spirituality at Crane Street, Pittsburgh. Its place would henceforth be outside official academia but in service of the worldwide church and its in-depth quest for faith formation in everyday life.

Except for an occasional elective course, I no longer tried to teach van Kaam's spirituality science. He was already into the sixth volume of his *Formative Spirituality* series[10] and was steadily moving into quantum physics, delineating his formation field theory with its five inter-dynamic, dialectical poles. I valued his theory but few had bought it! As I was now slipping almost exclusively into administration work, I decided to salvage something for spirituality by exploring at doctoral level the interface between spirituality and literature. I chose to do this at University College Dublin's English Department by focusing on the work of Patrick Kavanagh. I already knew the spiritual power in his metaphors and the exciting mystical thread that ran through his work. Van Kaam had taught me that 'the human spirit goes beyond, through, over things in their appearances'... and rests in the infinite Stillness that originates'. I pictured the poet 'dishevelled with shoes untied', slovenly in his outer appearance yet spiritually vibrant interiorly and capable of expressing his spirituality in exquisite lyricism. Symbolically, winter was over for me. The work of this poet heralded for me a new spring!

The old cranky spinster is dead
Who fed us cold flesh.
And in the green meadow
The maiden of Spring is with child
By the Holy Ghost.[11]

What spirituality lay unexplored in the work of this Monaghan poet? Evelyn Underhill's *Practical Mysticism* had ably demonstrated the mystical potential unconsciously present in ordinary people. I had studied her work closely and knew, with sound spiritual instinct, that Kavanagh had traces of a mystical imagination. But could I prove it? I was thoroughly familiar with his inner and outer landscapes, so I proceeded to apply a popular Dionysian methodology explicitated by Underhill to investigate this poet, who was poetically at home in 'the placeless heaven that's under all our noses'. By now I had almost lost touch with van Kaam's theory, but I knew he had given me sound tools by which to assess the spirituality of a poet.

Moving into a Second Relationship!

And so I moved into a second relationship! Kavanagh's genius deployed powerful metaphors to deal with the soul's hunger and longing. Earth, clay, weeds, seeds, sheaves and harvest spoke also of the cultivation of spiritual territory – the harvesting of life. The intimate local place, where love and life begin was, for him, the universal 'doorway to life'. Reading Kavanagh, researching his background, reclaimed for me my inheritance as an Irish woman, harvesting the nourishment that native landscape offers and penetrating with Kavanagh the hidden territories of the Irish soul. Glimpses of God peeked through the faces of primroses, bluebells and cut-away bogs. Light stared through the eyes of bridges, through the 'little window', that despite cramped circumstances 'lets in the sta'. This poet's philosophy dealt simultaneously with the cuts and bruises of life, yet found the courage to declare at the end: 'it is October over all my life'. Thus was born *The Mystical Imagination of Patrick Kavanagh: A Buttonhole in Heaven* (Columba Press, 1998), my small contribution to the study of spirituality. When a Department of Spirituality was founded in Milltown Institute in 2001, I was ready to return to van Kaam's formative spirituality theory but with Kavanagh also in tow. Sandra Schneiders' academic conversation around defining spirituality as an academic discipline was (and still is), in full swing, with Bernard McGinn, Mary Frolich, Elizabeth Liebert and Kees Waaijman also in full voice. It is the *déjà vu* experience *par excellence*!

Van Kaam has lost nothing in the interim, but is still that lone voice rarely quoted. The new explorers in the field of spirituality rarely mention his name. What a lesson from life! A writer can be so far ahead of his time that he can make himself invisible! Now in 2005, he is older and more fragile but has still completed his seven volume series of Formation Science and Anthropology, and has recently published with Dr Susan Muto, the first in their pending four-volume series on Formation Theology.[12] All who are indebted to this '21st century Aquinas!' pray that he will one day receive the credit he deserves. Though some of his students (including myself) abandoned teaching his theory, one never forgot his foundational formative process. That was for life. Schneiders may now be to the forefront in defining spirituality. All the experts quote her, but I cannot help wondering if she has even a slight suspicion that someone has ploughed these fields before her! As for me, I acknowledge the initial investment in my spirituality by van Kaam and believe that justice will ultimately be done.

Home at Last!

In 2001 Dr Bernadette Flanagan, Dr Jack Finnegan and I drafted a programme which was to become a two-year Masters

Programme in Applied Spirituality at the Milltown Institute. Within a year it was accredited by the State's Higher Education Training and Awards Council (HETAC) and is in line for recognition by the National University of Ireland (NUI). Though we did not particularly like the word 'Applied' we had to break loose from anything that would bind us to a course of studies that might be judged exclusively in terms of established theological criteria. We already had a programme in Classical Spirituality solidly rooted in the history of spirituality. This new programme was designed to engage critically with human experience, explore its depth-dimension in a self-implicating way and deploy an interdisciplinary research methodology. Research would be theologically informed, but also integrate insights from cognate human sciences. Academically, I was 'at home' in a flourishing Spirituality Department, the first of its kind in Ireland. Already students of spirituality acknowledge the shift of consciousness that has occurred for them through our teachings. They in turn by their research transform us and spur us to continually update ourselves spiritually and academically. And so, my path to spirituality has meandered, widened and deepened, from the foothills of Slieve Gullion, through France, to the US and back to my current spiritual home in Dublin. Here, in Milltown Institute, I am supported and inspired by friends, colleagues and students as I continue, these twenty years, to minister to the Word in a variety of ways. Writers as diverse as Kierkegaard, van Kaam, Muto, Underhill and Kavanagh have helped refashion and redefine my understanding of spirituality. I am still learning. My teaching has been sifted and transformed again and again by parents, family, teachers, colleagues, students and mentors at home and abroad. The poet Patrick Kavanagh reminds me gently that there is a little of 'October' left in my season of spirituality to deliver the final fruits of life's harvest.

Notes

1. The countryside of North Louth/South Armagh was known as 'The Fews', taking its name from Sliabh Fuaid, the original name for Sliabh Gullion.

2. Adrian van Kaam, *Religion and Personality* (Denville, N.J.: Dimension Books, 1968 and Epiphany Books, 1991) 41-43.

3. van Kaam, *The Demon and the Dove: Personality Growth through Literature* (Denville, N.J.: Dimension Books, 1963) 11, now available on CD Rom from the Epiphany Association.

4. *Religion and Personality* (1980 edition) vii.

5. *Formation Theology,* Vols I and II (Pittsburgh: Epiphany Books, 2003-2005).

6. See *Minding the Spirit: The Study of Christian Spirituality,* eds. Elizabeth Dreyer and Mark Burrows, (Baltimore and London: The John Hopkins University Press, 2005) where Sandra Schneiders, Bernard McGinn and Mary Frolich agree, with varying emphases, that spirituality as a discipline is rooted in 'lived human experience' (pp. 6, 32, 50, 65).

7. Søren Kierkegaard, *The Point of View for My Work as an Author,* trans. Walter Lowrie (New York: Harper Torchbooks, 1962).

8. Susan Muto, 'Reading the Symbolic Text: Some Reflections on Interpretation,' in *Creative Formation of Life and World* (Washington D.C.: University Press of America, 1982) 113-35. See also *Approaching the Sacred: Introduction to Spiritual Reading* (Denville, N.J.: Dimension Books, 1973) now available at www.epiphanyassociation.org.

9. Dermot A. Lane, *The Reality of Jesus* (Dublin and London: Veritas/Sheed and Ward, 1975, 1986).

10. There were 7 volumes published between 1989 and 2001 available at www.epiphanyassociation.org.

11. Quotation from 'April' and 'Auditors In' are from *The Complete Poems of Patrick Kavanagh* (Newbridge: The Goldsmith Press, 1972).

12. *Formation Theology Series* (2003-) available at www.epiphanyassociation.org.

2.

Theology in the Making

Mary Condren

From an early age, I considered that the question of *God* was either the most important or the most meaningless question in the world. Through a turbulent adolescence that questioned everything, I swung from atheism to mysticism (or maybe just hormonal intensity). I found some short-lived peace when I entered a Carmelite convent in England, barely aged twenty, but scripture study soon threw up even more questions. Reading the Synoptic Gospels (Matthew, Mark and Luke) opened up new interpretations of Jesus, religion, spirituality and of my vocation. My fate was now sealed, but where could I go?

In the Ireland of 1970, women were not admitted to the study of theology. However, through the good graces of Irishman, Anthony Hanson, Professor of Theology, I embarked on an undergraduate degree in theology, sociology and social anthropology at the University of Hull.

The combination was unusual, even for those times, but eminently sensible. Theology had been known as the *queen of the sciences* and, historically, theologians were expected to be highly educated cultural interpreters, able to speak intelligently across disciplines. But that was before the critiques of religion made by Marx, Freud and Nietzsche. I vividly remember a conversation with one of the sociology faculty. He had just complimented me on my essay on Karl Marx, but then asked: 'but don't you theologians believe in God or that people have souls?'

Entering into a theological degree by no means silenced my questioning. The feminist movement had just begun and exposés of the sordid history of religious misogyny quickly followed. The sheer scale of the attempts to silence, nullify, persecute and even murder women healers (witches), philosophers and mystics – except those who supported the misogyny – was breathtaking.

However, my torturous questions found a wider context. Articles such as 'Can a Male Saviour Save Women?', 'Beyond God the Father' or 'Jesus and the Liberation of Women' streamed forth. The question of gender was on the agenda at an interdenominational and inter-religious level and the exclusion of women from theological study and ordination in many traditions was now being seriously challenged.

Yet, while various traditions disagreed over major theological doctrines, or even over the question as to which deity should be considered supreme, they almost all agreed that sacrality and femaleness were at opposite poles. Women were subordinate, veiled in public and excluded from ordination. Their very existence appeared to be, in theological terms, and as Augustine had once said, 'a necessary evil' in the work of procreation.

However, the new language of feminist and liberation theology offered paradigms of interpretation that resonated with mine. I had long accepted that most images of God (especially some of my own) were idolatrous. Liberation theologian, José Miranda's treatment of St John's Gospel, *Marx and the Bible* was formative for my thinking. Miranda contended that if you want to know anything about God, *do* what Jesus did. Liberation theology's radical emphasis on praxis (the combination of belief and action) and increasing distaste for alienated metaphysical speculations resonated with me. They confirmed the teaching of the mystics – 'we know nothing about God', at the same time as they placed the quest for God within the struggle for human nobility and justice.

From all these sources I learned that Jesus, a radical revolutionary (like other major world religion founders such as the Buddha), consistently opposed the petrified forms of religion of his time. However, his interpreters, to universalise his message, often placed it within existing mythological systems, undermining the revolutionary potential and, incidentally, consolidating their own new power structures. That power structure was known as *patriarchy*, or later what Elisabeth Schüssler Fiorenza calls *kyriarchy* – the rule, not of loving fathers, but of dominating lords.

The Student Christian Movement

At Hull University I had become involved with the Student Christian Movement of Britain and Ireland (SCM), which became my parallel university for the next nine years. The SCM was committed to exploring the 'spiritual dimensions of political struggle'. On graduation, I worked for five years as editor of the SCM journal, *Movement* then an international journal of theology and politics.

Under those auspices I published and coordinated many events exploring various aspects of racism, imperialism, armaments, sexuality, class, radical education, socialism and what we then called Third World Development. Our combination of scholarship and irreverent humour brought such issues to life in the journal. My favourite was an issue entitled 'Why Men Priests?' prepared for the Lambeth Synod of 1977 in which we mounted tongue-in-cheek arguments against the ordination of men.

The feminist theological community quickly grew and I became a founder member and European co-ordinator of the Women's Project of the World Student Christian Federation (WSCF) in Europe, a position that took me to most European countries observing and resourcing the emerging feminist theological movement. The ordination of Lutheran women gave hope to the rest of us that our traditions would soon see the error of their ways. However, in 1976, the Vatican published its 'Declaration on the Ordination of Women' that firmly killed off any remaining illusions.

The Vatican had taken some feminist scholarship and twisted it to its own uses. '*Jesus a feminist? Yes, clearly he was.*' Nevertheless, they said, he had not ordained women and neither would they! The fact that Jesus ordained no one did not seem to matter. To their eternal credit some biblical scholars resigned when they saw the uses made of their consultative work. Theologians claimed that the Vatican risked heresy in some of its claims; others compiled brilliant compendia of theological responses exposing the shabby scholarship.

I was devastated and very much alone in the Ireland of 1976, but the emerging international sisterhood brought much needed solidarity. In 1976, the US Grail movement organised a Seminary Quarter for Women in Ohio, a six-week event for women in training for ministry. Several members – Elizabeth McGee, Janet Kalven, Mary Buckley and Mary Bohlen – aided by the Board of Global Ministries of the Methodist Church and the WSCF raised funds for me to attend. The following year, Monica Barnes, TD (Member of Parliament), and Mary Cullen from Maynooth collected funds for me to attend the Women's Ordination Conference (WOC) in Baltimore, Maryland.

Together with three or four thousand others from around the world, I heard inspiring addresses from many women of their call to priesthood and their faithfulness to vocation in spite of the restrictions placed by the Roman Catholic hierarchy. Equally inspiring, however, were the booths surrounding the conference, campaigning on many issues of social justice. Women involved with prisons, the homeless, prostitutes and base churches campaigned and educated through the conference proceedings.

Immediately afterwards, the American bishops held their annual conference in the Washington Hilton and I attended as a journalist. The contrast could not have been more stark. I sank down to my ankles in the plush carpets on the way up the stairs, only to find three booths at the top. The first recruited chaplains for the military; the second, for the army; the third sold bishops' clothing. The medium was the message.

It became painfully clear that questions of gender surrounded fundamental differences in understanding as to the nature of church and power. The radical women who had organised the ordination conference quickly came to the same conclusion. The 'add women and stir' approach to women's ordination was untenable; they called for nothing less than a complete ecclesial and theological revolution. In the short term, Womanchurch rather than women's ordination, was required. Many left *WOC* either to establish base *Womenchurch* communities or to seek ordination in other traditions.

Ireland

Back in Ireland, however, it was business as usual. (I had returned with *Movement* in 1976.) The *Irish Independent* interviewed me about the Vatican document, but the interview never saw the light of day. In the coming years, other newspapers commissioned articles for which they paid and never published. Clerical and religious abuse had yet to be widely exposed and a whistle blower like me was not welcome or even believed.

I had left Hull University with little intention of continuing in academic life. The University's inhumanity (it was partly funded through apartheid practices in South Africa), the response to the suicides of two friends and indeed my own experience as a working-class woman who had left school at fourteen had left me deeply suspicious about the academy's commitment to anything more than the perpetuation of its own privilege. And yet, given the political situation in Ireland, where a vicious combination of religion, politics and mythology had left thousands dead and many more orphaned or maimed, I now felt that my best future contribution could be made by analysing the connections between gender, violence, religion and spirituality.

Harvard Divinity School

In 1979 I was appointed a Research Associate in Women's Studies in the Women and Religion Programme at Harvard Divinity School. I went on to do an MA in Religion and Society at Boston College and a doctorate in theology at Harvard. In 1986 I returned to Ireland to complete my book *The Serpent and the Goddess: Women, Religion, and Power in Celtic Ireland*, published in 1989. In 1994 I finally completed my doctoral thesis (set in the Irish Rising of 1916): *The Role of Sacrifice in Constructing a Gendered Social Order and Gendered Systems of Representation*.

Throughout these works, the question of patriarchal violence and its legitimation through mythology, ritual practices and social constructions was foremost. Reading the texts, theological or Celtic, the masculinist bias was breathtaking. If Celtic mythology extolled the bravery of the warriors, patriarchal theology extolled a vicious version of God whose honour could be appeased only through the sacrifice of His Son.

The question formed itself: could it be that the male experience of being in the body has fundamentally shaped, designed and legitimated particular forms of theology and religious practice? The contemporary attitude towards women in fundamentalist religious regimes exposes the deep complicities. Veiled women, carefully guarded altars, restricted religious areas all these testify to the very tenuous hold that patriarchal forms exert on reality. In these religions, women and their bodies are *abject* – absolutely *Other*. Could it be that the unconscious process underlying the *Othering* of women through laws of purity, sacrificial rituals and their accompanying theologies also underlies the *Othering* process at the heart of warrior culture?

Could it be that the resulting one-sided spirituality, ritual, and symbol system has hugely distorted the message of their founders and the capacity of such religions to act positively in the world? If so, what analytical tools were needed to discern the way forward? Where did that leave the question of women?

The Future

Over the years people asked, 'Why do I bother with theology? Is there something wrong with my brain? Do I seriously believe in God?' In particular, my work as a feminist theorist seems incompatible with theology. 'Have I no self-respect, given the attitude of the churches to women?'

I sometimes wish there were simple answers to those questions, but very often the terms of the questions themselves have to be radically deconstructed. In a culture of entertaining sound-bites one is often best counseled to silence. To put it briefly: I have as much trouble as most with the dominant patriarchal definitions of God and soul. Yet, far from being irrelevant, I contend that defining and controlling such images and definitions of God and soul is where patriarchy most blatantly exerts its power and privilege over the social imaginary.

Today the social imaginary has radically shifted from the churches to the battlefields, virtual and otherwise. Religion and politics continue an uneasy dance mutually supporting their various forms of patriarchal power that serve to keep their respective constituencies in infantile relationships of dependency, at the same time as they exercise a political dominance that threatens the future of civilisation.

The promises of the Enlightenment have not been realised. The huge layers of irrationality obvious under consumer capitalism, the proliferation of hard-core pornography, the ongoing violence against and objectification of women should leave no one under any illusion that *religion has gone away*. If anything, the mass retrograde movements of fascism, Nazism, communism, together with the more recent ethnic cleansing wars of Eastern Europe have shattered any remaining Enlightenment optimism.

The other side of this picture, however, and the one taken up by those postmodernist thinkers such as Julia Kristeva and Luce Irigaray, who most influence my academic work, is the enduring power of religions to shape, colonise, direct or otherwise make use of some fundamental human propensities. If humanity is to have a future, the energies that once were given religious expression had better be taken account of, shaped, modified and contained so that their political and social expression is better anticipated and directed toward humanistic ends.

Of course, this is a very tall order and one can never predict the outcome of any intervention in such matters. Equally, however, in the light of our human history to date, we must be able to identify elements in various religious traditions that have made for peace, tolerance and justice, and those that fostered their opposites. We must interrogate the interconnections between religion and violence and, specifically, the relationship between gender, religion and violence, which today in an international context (and much to the surprise of many intellectuals) has taken centre stage.

Institute for Feminism and Religion

Since 1995, as director of the Institute for Feminism and Religion, such questions have formed our focus. The Institute was set up to 'explore a prophetic approach to feminism and religion, inclusive of many traditions and the emerging consciousness in Ireland'. We have done this by providing opportunities for women to reclaim religion by engaging theoretically and experientially with the issues of feminist theology, ethics, spirituality and ritual.

Working on a shoestring budget, but with the aid of many volunteers, over the years we have put on lecture and seminar series and revisited ancient festivals such as the ancient festival of *Imbolc* or Brigit, Goddess and Saint. In her spirit we attempt to bridge the gaps between pagan and Christian, rich and poor, slave and free, by cultivating her chosen virtue: *mercy.*

To date, our Institute has focussed on women, hoping, in the immortal words of Methodist theologian, Nelle Morton, that we 'hear each other into speech'. However, the interrelationships between questions of gender, theology and violence make it imperative that both women and men engage in serious dialogue on these issues. In any future third-level work in theology, the question of gender must move from the margins to the mainstream to become, along with the critiques of Marx, Freud and Nietzsche, a crucial variable in any authentic discernment. Here are some of the crucial issues.

1. Gender, Religion and the Social Contract

In the early days of feminism we happily lived with the illusion that men were violent and women were their victims. Today, that analysis is much more complicated. No one denies the reality of patriarchal violence, but now we also focus on women's role in forming and shaping the social contract. If white Western women are oppressed and colonised, they, in their turn, oppress and colonise (through anonymous and sanitised capitalism mechanisms) women and children in the Two-Thirds world. If men externalise their violence on others, women often internalise violence on themselves, or project it onto other women through female horizontal violence. Religions often provide potent forums and ideologies for this to happen.

2. Women's Souls

Whereas the Early Fathers wondered whether women *had* souls, for contemporary feminists, cultivating *women's souls* is a practical task rather than a theoretical question. Luce Irigaray speaks of women's 'divine becoming'. Jungian theorist, Marion Woodman, speaks of the 'quest for embodied spirit'. Others speak of the search for 'The Goddess'. All believe that centuries of misogyny and discrimination can only be redressed by means of spiritual, cultural, artistic, representational, and bodily practices that serve actively to *cultivate* women. Alongside such practices must also come the active recuperation of symbols and sources of authentic female agency, especially those that have been erased or repressed for over two-thousand years.

3. Mercy Not Sacrifice

Throughout my theological work, a recurring cry of the prophets and of Jesus resounded: 'I desire mercy not sacrifice'. Yet the religions established in Jesus' name have used sacrificial rituals to delineate clearly gender relations.

The call for mercy is the call of the prophets. The call for sacrifice is that of the priests. Ironically, prophets in the major world traditions have more in common with their prophetic counterparts in other traditions than they have with priests in their own. How can we further elaborate on this prophetic potential to develop new grounds for inter-religious dialogue?

Mercy radically cuts through the *Othering* capacities of all religions. Mercy forces one to re-integrate the split-off parts of the self and their projection into excluded *Others*. The call for mercy must, therefore, be at the heart of any gendered approach to theology that takes violence seriously into account.

Conclusion

If theology was once the 'queen of the sciences,' today, her dress is bedraggled; her demeanour, subservient; her reputation, tarnished. Having entered into a sacred marriage with the political powers of this world (gaining immunity from equality legislation as a reward), theology is now sidelined, ridiculed and feminised. Effectively, theology has become unable to challenge the onward march of a patriarchal predatory power that is wreaking havoc on the earth and its children.

Given its loss of social status, women are now admitted to the study of theology. Indeed, in many schools they comprise the majority of students. However, the theological agendas still function on the 'add women and stir' approach, as though two-thousand years of misogyny has not irrevocably shaped the discipline. New wine now requires new wineskins. Only a genuine dialectic between the embodied spirits of women and men working as equals and reaching together towards authenticity and integrity can now fertilise and re-invigorate the discipline.

And what about my Marxist professor's question: 'Do we believe in God or have souls?' For many, the words 'God' or 'Soul' function as nouns. For others, they are verbs. For me, the words 'God' and 'soul' are questions I give to my attempts to live with integrity. I suspect that any answers will be found, not in metaphysical speculation, but in ethics and praxis. Furthermore, an attempt to concretise, control or petrify divine imagery closes off the questions and consolidates relations of power.

The prophetic call for *mercy* pushes one further and further into the essence of one's existence. And at a time when religious certainty firmly armours those who keep their fingers on the nuclear buttons, prophets belong in the deserts, perhaps the only place where the still voice can yet be heard.

3.

An Accidental Theologian

James Corkery

I was an ambitious young man. At around the age of seven, when asked by an aunt what I wanted to be when I grew up, I stifled my indignation at the question – in my view, I had already grown up – and responded unhesitatingly: 'either an engine-driver or the Pope'. That was in 1961 and now, four and a half decades later, I concede that neither of these dreams is likely to be realised. Nonetheless, I observe that the interests that lay embedded in each of them have remained my lifelong companions and, while I have not yet driven an engine, I have certainly been driven by them, pursued them and indeed can still burst into a sprint at the promise of catching a mere glimpse of one. As for the papacy, while my ambitions have notably lessened, the interest in religion that they surreptitiously embodied has influenced greatly, and continues to enrich, my lifestory. So all is not lost!

A last-minute decision made by my parents – again, when I was at that fateful age of seven – probably influenced the course of my theological life more than anything else. I was sent to the Jesuit school in my hometown of Limerick, where I remained, contentedly, until finally completing my secondary education in 1972. It was a happy, unpretentious school where, I learned quickly and to my delight, you could say anything you wished as long as you could back it up. The ethos was one of respect for individuals and for genuine inquiry; most of the teachers had imbibed it; and, if there was a strong emphasis placed on examinations and the achievement of good results, I never particularly noticed it or – as a lifelong friend still reminds me – I never really allowed it to interfere with my enjoyment of, and curiosity about, life. My former Latin and religion teacher, who is now almost ninety and lives in a Jesuit retirement home, asks me whenever I visit: 'Have you come to apologise?' He does not seem to mind that I can never quite bring myself to do so and he even grudgingly admits that teaching my class gave him a lightness of step many a morning, for at least we were 'a lively bunch'.

Of religion classes I remember little and, when I attempt to suggest that I was always attentive in them, that same teacher snorts: 'Yes, to other things'. But he will admit that I sometimes piped up from my distractions (the completion of homework in other subjects, for example) to join a discussion on God's goodness in the face of evil, on the dignity of the human person or even on the historicity of the Gospels. Apparently I usually took the side that was 'friendly' to God and religion and, if memory serves me correctly, I robustly took on the fairly persuasive class atheist on more than one occasion. Clearly I was interested in theological questions from an early age and I remember this interest being accompanied by, perhaps even being the product of, two convictions that I never remember *not* having: that human beings are inherently good and valuable; and that the world in which we live, for all its imperfections, is enveloped, upheld, undergirded by a kind of attentive benevolence that will not see it stuck – will not leave it abandoned – as it unfolds in all its vicissitudes. I presume I assimilated these beliefs by a kind of osmosis through the ordinary love of my family and friends, the ethos of the school and certain 'antecedent inclinations' (John Henry Newman) of my own with which I was fortunate to be blessed by temperament and disposition from an early age.

Embarking on Life's Journey

In 1972, armed with my basic education and convictions, I embarked on the journey of life. I joined the Jesuits at that time, not really knowing what I was letting myself in for but having a feeling that I could not shake off – and, believe me I had tried to shake it off! – that this might be the way for me, and that I had better give it a try. Thirty-three years later, after many ups and downs, I am still giving it a try, armed no less with the basic optimism of my early convictions, but also, now, with the realism that life brings and the 'hermeneutic of suspicion' that inevitably develops over years of critical reflection and reading. I thought I would end up a school teacher – I had been very happy during a teaching stint between 1979 and 1981 – but once I began theology studies in 1981 a suspicion I had had as a social science student (in University College, Dublin, from 1974 to 1977) and as a student of philosophy (in Munich, from 1977 to 1979) that I would end up an academic gradually ripened to a decision and a mission. And so, from 1981 to 1991, I completed bachelor, licentiate and doctoral degrees in theology, the first at the Milltown Institute of Theology and Philosophy in Dublin and the other two at The Catholic University of America in Washington, DC. My life had acquired shape; and theology was to be at its centre.

But Why Theology?

From the earliest times – long before I really noticed it – theology was everywhere. Already as a schoolboy I had been immersed in a way of seeing things that made it easier to be aware that I lived in a *milieu divin*. I acquired this awareness courtesy, really, of Saint Ignatius Loyola's spirituality of 'finding God in all things'. I did not see that this finding of God was graced, that it depended on a kind of 'already having been found'. Nor did I see that my convictions that human beings are inestimably valuable and that the world is 'borne up' by a silent, supporting benevolence, expressed the bible's belief that we are made in the divine image (Genesis 1: 26–27) and Christian faith's understanding that we are created and redeemed in love. Yet these convictions guided my inquiry and later, as a postgraduate student specialising in theological anthropology, I came to appreciate how Leonardo Boff's notion of 'transparence' (the invisible 'shining through' the visible in a sacramental world) and Karl Rahner's 'supernatural existential' (God's universal offer of saving grace to all) expressed in theological language what I had 'always already known'.

There was more. As a very young Jesuit student I had been trained initially in the social sciences and this led me to discover the social and cultural rootedness of my thinking and to gain an appreciation of how, when I attempted to locate myself in other social contexts and to see things from different, less socially privileged viewpoints, my bourgeois convictions were challenged. They were challenged, too, by developments in church and theology. In theology during the 1970s, the *social* was exploding onto the stage. It gained expression not least in texts such as *Justice in the World* from the 1971 Synod of Bishops; and in Decree Four of the Jesuit General Congregation of 1974/1975, sketching the contours of a committed faith to which the promotion of justice integrally belonged. And then there were the inspiring works of the Latin American liberation theologians. So as students we came to see that we were doing our theology in contexts of social inequality and injustice. Categories like 'social sin' gradually became central to my own thoughts as I saw that the problems of society – massive unemployment, the widening gap between rich and poor, the continued subjugation of women – made the preaching of the Christian Gospel hollow if it had no effect on justice in society. So a criterion of true theology had to be: does it promote justice? That focus on Gospel (or Kingdom) justice shifted my reflection away from 'social sin', which had already been striking me as a bit too negative, and towards 'social grace', i.e. grace in community, society and history. Prompted by an Irish Jesuit, Tim Hamilton, I read around that time an article on societal grace by Thomas Clarke, a New York Jesuit, in which Clarke pointed out that we humans live on the *intra, inter-* and *trans-* personal levels; and so grace, if it builds on human nature, must surely be found on those levels also: within persons, between persons in relationship and at the heart of communities and societies. This idea excited me and crystallised into something I became interested in pursuing.

The Social-Structural Dimensions of Grace and 'Dis-grace'

That pursuit began consciously in 1984, the year I was ordained a priest and moved to Washington DC. Searching around for a thesis topic for my licentiate in theology, I came upon an article written by Erich Schrofner in 1980 on grace and experience in Rahner and Boff. It pointed out that, while the *nouvelle théologie* and even the theology of Karl Rahner had had the individual as their main point of interest, Leonardo Boff's theology of grace was marked, in a way hitherto unknown, by the themes of history and society.[1] Attracted by Boff's emphasis, I eventually wrote a licentiate thesis on the social–structural dimensions of grace and 'dis-grace' in his theology.[2] I was guided by Father Avery Dulles, who, not long before, had written an article on the meaning of faith considered in relationship to justice and had explored, as a form of faith alongside the more traditional ones – intellectualist and fiducial, performative faith.[3] So Dulles was sympathetic to my interests, even if not as 'liberationist' as I; and his guidance permitted me remarkable freedom and independence.

The work on Boff provided me with a language for speaking about grace not only in social and historical terms, but also, and more foundationally, in a highly experiential way. I found points to critique, of course, and I even consulted the Congregation for the Doctrine of the Faith's *Notification* (1985) on Boff's book, *Church, Charism and Power* (1981) that the Congregation had issued during the time I was writing my thesis. Although the focus of Boff's book was ecclesiological, not anthropological, it did lead me to read the Congregation's writings on liberation theology, above all its 1984 and 1986 *Instructions*; and these led me to an article by the Prefect of the Congregation, Cardinal Joseph Ratzinger, in which he presented the 'anthropological vision' of the 1986 *Instruction*. After that, the step to examining Ratzinger's own anthropological vision was not distant, especially since I had good German (since my years in Munich, where he was Archbishop at the time) and could read his many – at that time largely untranslated – writings. And so, for my doctoral dissertation, I came to write on the relationship between anthropology and soteriology in Joseph Ratzinger's theology, the soteriological focus being added to the anthropological because Ratzinger had expressed concern that, in liberation theology, a rather materialist anthropology and a too-immanent notion of salvation went hand-in-hand. Thus one can see: the move from Boff to Ratzinger was not a matter of examining two theological 'extremes' but rather an attempt to investigate an overall conversation about salvation and humanity that was taking place in theology and church at the time. Through my research into Ratzinger I gradually came to see that his roots in the theologies of Saints Augustine and Bonaventure shed much light on his opposition to theological approaches that give primacy – or at least 'equiprimacy' – to praxis. Because of that research, I remain interested today in the roots – the historical allegiances, if you like – of contemporary theologians because these appear to me to affect, quite profoundly, their attitudes to contemporary questions.

Underlying Theological Vision

What I have said of other theologians applies to me too, of course! So, what about my own roots and inclinations? These surfaced spontaneously as I began to teach and write theology on my return to Dublin, and the Milltown Institute, in 1991. Asked in 1992 to teach fundamental theology, I instinctively reached for the more 'ascending' approach of Rahner and Lonergan than for the 'descending' one of Ratzinger. The latter begins, always, with that of which 'the faith' speaks; but my spontaneous inclination was always to begin, at least methodologically, with human experience and to attempt (Rahner-like, Tillich-like?) to correlate it with the rich tradition of the faith. When asked to teach theological anthropology ('grace') in 1993, I found myself returning to Boff's emphasis on grace as experienced (for all the nuancing that is involved in saying so) and – the more I delved into the patristic and medieval traditions – leaning more towards Aquinas' approach to grace, and to the goodness (despite sin) of the created human nature upon which grace built, rather than towards the trajectory represented by Augustine and Bonaventure, which seemed unduly pessimistic about the effects of sin and unduly cautious about ascribing excellence to human nature. I have remained, broadly speaking, more persuaded by 'the healthy theology of Aquinas' and the 'realistic, optimistic perspective' it seems to embody[4] than by the other perspectives that I mentioned above. Through a decade and a half of teaching in such areas as fundamental theology, grace, theological method, liberation theologies, the theology of suffering and, more recently, theology in dialogue with postmodern culture(s), I have seemed to operate spontaneously with an incarnational vision of God's interactions with the world as allowing wheat and weeds (see Matthew 13:24–30) to grow together – to be sifted and discerned by theological detectives of grace along the way – but not to be cut down as they mature. There is a double recognition here: that purification will always be required if any human creation is to flourish; but also that, in our human co-creating, God will, in due time, 'give the increase' (see 1 Corinthians 3:6–7). It may be argued that this vision is a bit too optimistic, yet it cannot be declared that it is without warrant in the Christian tradition.

A Look into the Future

My theological interests and questions today are in continuity with the story that has been told so far. In the last half dozen years or so, my reflections have turned more towards culture: the challenge to Christian faith of postmodern cultures; the relationship between spirituality and culture the divine (graced) and anti-divine (sinful) dimensions of cultures, such as we experience them in Europe and North America. In a forthcoming sabbatical I wish – as well as penning a few pieces on Joseph Ratzinger that have been asked for as a result of recent events in his life – to engage mainly in bringing research that I have carried out for postgraduate courses in the social dimensions of grace into dialogue with some emerging postmodern theologies that have highlighted the challenges that are facing committed Christian faith in contemporary postmodern cultural settings. These cultural *milieux* are marked by the presence of a plurality of religions and by an eclectic approach to spiritualities, thought-forms and patterns of living that raise disturbing questions about Christian identity. Such questions interest me because, at root, I seem to be a fundamental theologian who is concerned, no matter what the cultural and social circumstances, to tell the Christian story in an engaging way, thereby giving an account of the hope that is in me (see 1 Peter 3:15) and that can be in us. In this sense I see theology as a mission: the gift of understanding things so that they can be handed on. Occasionally I worry that the drive – essentially apostolic, 'missionary' – to render Christian faith intelligible and attractive is an indication that I have not made it into the 'postmodern' era, but remain something like a 'reconstructed modernist'. Then I remember that it is *this* world, this fragmented postmodern world, that God so loves (see John 3:16) and that seems to make possible again the mission of being a detective of grace who seeks to uncover the seeds of the Word in contemporary circumstances, even if the latter can be seen to bear many traces of elements that are inimical to the Christian Gospel and way of life. Like the theologies of mission that flourished in the wake of Vatican II, I work from the assumption that God is 'always already present' and that my task, as a theologian, is to help uncover that benevolent presence and to tease out how it may be attempting to bring life to people today. Saint Paul is the inspiration here as he recognises that the brothers and sisters at Phillipi live among a 'deceitful and underhand brood' (Deuteronomy 32:5) and yet he can say to them, whom he encourages to live differently: 'you will shine in the world like bright stars because you are offering it the word of life' (Philippians 2:15–16). Theology, as a Christian ministry, is meant to shine like a star too – to offer hope and to present the word of life, often amid pathways of death.

Concluding Reflections

I never expected to become a theologian and I would not have survived and grown as one if the element of mission were missing. I had assumed I would end up a secondary school teacher or a missionary in Asia, like Francis Xavier perhaps; but hardly a theologian. However, during the long years of Jesuit studies, I was overtaken unexpectedly by a kind of joy in understanding that made me an enthusiastic student, eventually a hard worker and finally even what others began to call a 'natural' academic. Though I had many personal struggles, study was never one of them. It brought light, life and lightness; and it helped me to make sense of things. A family member remarked to me once that, if he asked as many questions as I did, he would lose his faith, but that if I asked as few as he did, I would lose mine! Attempting to make sense of things is a worthy human undertaking and it brings great joy – and it leads, spontaneously, to a desire to enable others to find the same joy. If I had any dream for Ireland in the coming decades, it would be that the sphere of theological discourse would widen, that greater numbers of people would be involved – and would be publicly supported to be involved – in theological conversation and that it would become possible for theology to move increasingly beyond the boundaries often set for it by a fearful and worried church and by a society that tends to relegate religion entirely to the private sphere. Theology, as I have been saying, has a mission to make sense of things. In the great human questions of the day it does not belong on the sidelines.

From all I have written, it is clear that I see theology as involving an integration of three A's: the autobiographical, the academic and the apostolic. Life-chances and personal inclination made me a theologian (the autobiographical); study taught me to think – and to value thinking (the academic); and the enterprise of doing theology would have made little sense if I could not have made theological sense to others (the apostolic). Theology is not an end in itself – 'here's to pure theology, may it never be of any use to anyone!' I am reminded here of a story. A Jesuit and former teacher of mine once said he would give up all his theology and philosophy if he could play the accordion (the latter being so practical for gathering people and bringing them life). However, he visibly baulked when I suggested that he give up mathematics. He suddenly saw that mathematics meant everything to him, not because, in itself, it was the be-all and end-all, but rather because of what it enabled him to do. He was a wonderful teacher; and it was what he was able to do with young people through mathematics that gave him lasting joy in the subject. It is the same for me with theology: I would give it all up in the morning if it were not an instrument for enlivening the minds and hearts of students and colleagues and for enabling our hearts to burn within us a little more as we walk along the road together (see Luke 24:32).

Notes

1. See Erich Schrofner, 'Gnade und Erfahrung bei Karl Rahner und Leonardo Boff: Zwei Wege gegenwärtiger Gnadentheologie,' in *Geist und Leben* 53:4 (August 1980) 266-80.

2. For an overview of what I discovered see James Corkery SJ, 'The Social Dimensions of Grace and 'Dis-grace' in the Theology of Leonardo Boff,' in *Bobolanum* 6 (1995) 92-119.

3. Avery Dulles SJ, 'The Meaning of Faith Considered in Relationship to Justice,' in John C. Haughey (ed.), *The Faith that Does Justice: Examining the Christian Sources for Social Change,* Woodstock Studies 2 (New York/Ramsey, NJ: Paulist Press, 1977) 10-46.

4. I have borrowed the phrases in parentheses from a recent (and delightful) book by Thomas F. O'Meara, OP. See *A Theologian's Journey* (New York/Mahwah, NJ: Paulist Press, 2002) 27.

4.

Turning Points on a Journey

Donal Dorr

Have You Been 'Saved'?

Certain key events in my life stand out as turning points on my theological journey. The first of these came while I was a seminarian, ploughing through the boring and irrelevant courses of pre-Vatican II dogmatic and moral theology. I went to work in England one summer and, finding it impossible to get a place to stay, I was happy to accept the invitation of a fellow-worker to stay in his house. He turned out to be a born-again Baptist, a former rough-living sailor who had a dramatic conversion experience and knew he was 'saved'. He probably saw in me a potential convert. Dialogue with him led me to a kind of conversion. I became intensely interested in the notion that one could have an *experience* of God's saving grace – an idea that was quite strange to me and which found little basis in the neo-Scholastic theology I had learned.

Not surprisingly, then, when I came in the following year to do a postgraduate degree in theology, I chose for my doctoral dissertation the topic 'The Wesleyan Doctrine of Sin and Salvation'. Fascinated by John Wesley's account of his dramatic conversion – and the various interpretations he gave of it – I was led to study religious psychology, starting with William James' *The Varieties of Religious Experience*. Gradually I came to see the inadequacy of the neo-scholastic theology of grace in which I had been schooled. This led me to seek within our Catholic tradition for some writings on spiritual feelings and related topics. My most important discovery was an article on the experience of grace by Karl Rahner in which he challenged the neo-Scholastic view that grace, being supernatural, could not be experienced.

'Giants at my Shoulder'

Ever since 1961 Rahner has been one of the two 'giants at my shoulder', always bringing me fresh and exciting new theological ideas – even though I have doubts about the validity of key aspects of his early philosophical work. For me as a missionary it was very liberating to adopt Rahner's view that human history as a whole is salvation history and that every people has its own salvation history; and to see the Judeo-Christian tradition as a key to understanding this wider history rather than as the one and only 'sacred history'. I was particularly taken by Rahner's account of Christ's divinity as the complete fulfilment of his humanity – with all its implications about *our* humanity. Many years later I attempted to apply this in a more readable form in my books *Divine Energy* (1996) and *Mission in Today's World* (2000).

In writing my dissertation on Wesley I was inspired by the ecumenical thrust of Hans Küng's major study of Karl Barth, which had been published shortly beforehand. It was easy to find 'Catholic' elements in the thinking of Wesley, even though he rejected 'Papism' as he understood it; and his emphasis on Christian experience was a helpful challenge to the pre-Vatican II Catholic theology. All this had a profound effect on my later theological thinking. Feeling fully at home in my Catholic tradition (despite being disturbed by the current excessive zeal of its official guardians), I am eager to enrich – and, if necessary, to correct – my Catholic spirituality and theology by incorporating key elements of the Protestant, Anglican and Pentecostal traditions. It is a matter of deep regret for me that I have not yet delved into Orthodox theology and spirituality.

When I finished my formal theological studies I went on to do a postgraduate degree in philosophy and then joined the staff of the philosophy department in University College, Cork. I thank God that I had the opportunity to teach philosophy for four years before going on to teach theology. I became enthused about Teilhard de Chardin; and some of Heidegger's writings opened up new territory for me, particularly on 'the gods', as distinct from God. At this time, too, I was very influenced by Rosemary Haughton's writings about grace in experiential terms. I was fortunate that my brother Frank introduced me to Bernard Lonergan's *Insight* in 1964 and kept me in touch over many years with the group who were exploring Lonergan's writings and his developing thought. Lonergan is the other 'giant who sits at my shoulder' alongside Rahner – but he fulfils a rather different role. Where Rahner's insights sparkle and stimulate me, Lonergan's philosophy of knowledge provides a solid basis on which all my theology rests. His *Method in Theology* and other later writings provide the palatable and exciting icing on the rather heavy cake which is *Insight*.

Over the years, my theology has been enormously enriched by dialogue with my sister, Ben, and my brothers Noel and Frank. One of the chapters in my recent book, *Time for a Change* (2004), is largely a popularising of material written some years ago by my sister. She and my brothers (along with some close friends) have shared ideas with me and put me in touch with sources and approaches which I would not have otherwise discovered. My writing on issues of justice in the world were given some measure of realism by endless dialogue and argument with my brother Noel, who was engaged as a diplomat in facing these issues at the United Nations and nearer home. Then there was the life-giving experience of being loved and of loving in return, which put to the test my understanding of celibacy and saved me (I hope) from the danger of becoming dried up.

Providence

In the 1960s the word 'spirituality' was scarcely ever used in the circles in which I moved. But over the past thirty years the word – and the reality – has become more and more central to my life, and it is now the source from which I try to draw my theology. My present-day spirituality is rooted in my childhood experience in my family and the community in the West of Ireland village where I was born.

Life in the village of Foxford centred around the woollen mills founded in 1891 by Sister Arsenius Morrough-Bernard. She had a total trust in providence, so she named her enterprise 'The Providence Woollen Mills'. This explicit sense of providence became part of the atmosphere of the village. It was shared by my father who started work tending the spinning machines on the factory floor when he was sixteen years old and who eventually rose to become the textile designer for the mills. My mother was a nurse who in 1932 came to look after Mother Morrough-Bernard in her final illness. Her trust in providence matched that of her patient. No wonder, then, that a central feature my own spirituality has been a strong sense of God's loving and providential care.

This trust was severely tested in the ferment of new theology during and after Vatican II, when many of us found it hard to find room for God's action in a secular world 'explained' by science. However, Lonergan's magisterial clarification of the teaching of Aquinas on grace (mediated through the work of the Irish Jesuit John Hyde) gave me a satisfying account of how human freedom (as well as human science) can be reconciled with God's action in the world.

Grace in Other Cultures

In 1973 came the second major turning-point in my life, when I went to work in Nigeria. Those early years in Africa were a time when my spirituality moved largely from my head to my heart. Working in a huge slum parish on the outskirts of Lagos, I came in touch with the everyday experience of poor and exploited people. This gave an experiential grounding to the exciting liberation theology which for me up to then had remained in the realm of theory. It also put me in touch with the world of African primal or traditional religion – particularly in relation to the role of spirits and the centrality of healing. The charismatic movement, which was sweeping Nigeria at that time, related quite well to this tangibly spiritual world of African people; it led me to be much more spontaneous in prayer and introduced me to the practice of praying for healing with people.

At this time, too, some of the Holy Child Sisters with whom I was working introduced me to the rediscovered Ignatian spirituality – not the legalistic version of my seminary days but a vibrantly experiential spirituality focussed on 'discernment on spirits'. It was a real 'eye-opener' for me to discover that I could search for guidance from the Spirit by exploring my own spiritual feelings and experiences. All this linked up organically with my earlier studies of religious psychology and of John Wesley's spirituality. It also put flesh on what I had learned from Rahner about the experience of grace. What a relief it was to escape from what I call the 'upstairs-downstairs' neo-Scholastic theology of grace, where the whole realm of the supernatural was seen as being 'upstairs', beyond the realm of experience.

During the 1970s I had the opportunity to spend some months with my missionary colleagues who were working in the slum areas around Sao Paulo in Brazil. While there I took time to study the local spiritist or *Macumba* cults, called *Umbanda* and *Candomble*. These were of particular interest to me because their divinities or *orisha* were the very divinities of the Yoruba peoples around Lagos where I had been living; they had been taken to Brazil by the African slaves who proceeded to amalgamate them with the Christian saints of the Portuguese colonial power. It was remarkable how these spiritist cults flourished and attracted people of all ethnic backgrounds, who came to them looking for healing and for guidance in their lives. This made me more aware than ever of the importance of experienced religion. It was out of these African and Brazilian experiences that I wrote my first book, *Remove the Heart of Stone*, published in 1978.

Freire: Another Kind of Conversion

Just as important as my discovery of experienced religion was a third turning point which came in 1975. Having lectured in philosophy and theology for ten years I had become quite disillusioned with that whole style of teaching – one where I tried to transmit theories about God and the world in lecture form to students with whom I had only a minimal personal relationship. My efforts to improve things by organising discussion groups had left both my students and myself still very much 'in our heads', spinning ideas which we could not be sure were rooted in reality.

The resolution of this personal crisis came in the form of a kind of conversion experience which took place in the most unlikely of places – a desert in the north of Kenya. There I came in touch for the first time with an approach called 'the psycho-social method'. It is a style of adult education and empowerment based primarily on the work of Paulo Freire, liberally mixed with group-work skills involving listening and facilitation exercises and planning techniques. For me, it was an experience of 'coming home', because it met my hunger to communicate with people at a deep level on key issues of faith and justice. It changed my whole life. I practically gave up lecturing and began instead to facilitate groups of all kinds. I got involved in organising and running development workshops and leadership training in several African countries as well as in Ireland. We worked with Christians and Muslims and with people who were alienated from formal religion, focussing on economic and political development, but always integrating the spiritual dimension. It was quite thrilling to see downtrodden people find their voice and begin to work effectively for change. How exciting it was to discover that 'things can be different', and to believe that the leaders we were training could play an important role in the liberation and healing of our broken and unjust world!

In 1980 I took up a research fellowship in Maynooth on the theology of development. This meant I spent four years studying development economics and related topics in politics, culture and religion. My research – combined with my continuing work 'on the ground' – gave rise eventually to four books on the relationship between spirituality and justice. By the 1990s the emphasis began to shift a little as the ecological issue came to the fore. And, because of my experience in living in different cultures, whenever I was organising or running workshops about development or justice or ecology, I always highlighted the cultural dimensions of these issues.

Spiritual Growth, Therapy and Intuition

Within the past few years I have concentrated more on workshops where the focus is on spiritual growth and the development of intuition and creativity in individuals and in teams. This latest change of focus came partly as a result of another key turning point in my spiritual journey. In 1981 my brother Frank persuaded me to take part in a powerful multi-dimensional workshop called 'The Hero's Journey'. This led me to get involved in a wide variety of 'human growth' workshops and eventually to a long-term commitment to personal therapy of the Jungian kind.

My concentration on personal spiritual growth arises also from my growing interest as a missionary in exploring the strands of spirituality that have been coming to the fore as more and more people in Ireland become disillusioned with the Church and formal religions. Most of these new aspects or elements of spirituality are drawn from one or all of four main sources: 'deep ecology', feminism, Eastern religions, and New Age practices.

All four of these come together in spiritual centres such as the Findhorn Foundation in northern Scotland, where I have spent time on several occasions. The most valuable 'tool' I have taken from there is a workshop called 'The Transformation Game', which comes in a variety of versions. I have used it quite a lot, expanding and adapting it into a retreat format, which incorporates significant periods of silence and some sacred dance and liturgy. What I have found particularly helpful is a more specialised adaptation of this process called 'Frameworks for Change'. This was originally designed for people in managerial positions in the business world. I have used a somewhat more overtly religious version of this workshop dozens of times with the leadership teams of religious congregations – mainly as a process to put them in touch with movements of the Spirit and to help them in discernment. I find it is also a very useful tool for surfacing and handling troublesome issues and developing a team spirit – and more particularly for developing creativity and people's intuitive powers. All this provides me with interesting and exciting 'raw material' for subsequent theological reflection. More importantly, the excitement of seeing people's minds inspired and their hearts opened in such workshops nourishes my own faith and hope – and convinces me that the message of Jesus is meaningful in today's world.

In 1997 I undertook a three-year training programme in Process Oriented Psychology – a model of therapy and group work which borrows elements from Jungian and Gestalt psychology and also draws on Daoism and shamanism. I find it very congenial to my understanding of facilitation because of the way in which it integrates the spiritual with the psychological and sensitises people to the movements of the Spirit in themselves and in the world. For me, that lies at the heart of what theology should be about today. For nearly two-thousand years Western theology failed to pay adequate attention to the work of the Spirit. Now at last, just when people are becoming disillusioned with institutions, we are rediscovering the Spirit. It is an exciting time to be a theologian.

The theology in which I am interested is a reflection on spiritual experience, my own and that of others whose journey I have shared in some degree. I find that I become stimulated – even at times inspired – when I am intensely engaged with people in a workshop on justice, mission or any other aspect of their spiritual search. Sometimes I have the opportunity to feed back to the group some of the insights which our work together has sparked off in me. In other workshops I find it more appropriate to stay in the facilitator role. Later, however, I can 'gather the fragments', as Jesus told his friends to do, and perhaps eventually put them together in a readable form. For many years now, all of my books and writings – even those which required much research – have been attempts to share with a wider audience the fruits of such real-life experience. I am grateful to have what Patrick Kavanagh calls 'a holy hearing audience'; and I find that my theology not only nourishes my own faith but also helps me to share with others my faith in the God whom Jesus reveals as caring for every hair on our heads, and in the Spirit who leads and inspires us moment by moment.

5.

Theology in the Making

Seán Fagan

In the mid-1980s in Rome I was involved in a five-day live-in seminar on theology/missiology with about 120 participants. During the coffee break after my lecture I was approached by an African religious sister, a very bright theologian whom I had not previously met. After commenting on some of the ideas I had presented, she surprised me with the spontaneous and beautiful compliment, 'You must have had a wonderful mother'. I had never mentioned my family or background, but I had to admire her intuition and admit the truth of her statement. She had touched a very deep level of my being, reminding me of a truth that has been at the very centre of my consciousness since I first devoted myself to theology. It has to do with the dynamic relationship between theology and the 'real world', the ordinary everyday world of all God's holy people. Dominican theologian Marie-Dominique Chenu put it very simply:

> The theologian, unlike the philosopher, works on history. His 'givens' are neither the natures of things nor their eternal forms, but events ... And events are always tied to time ... This, not the abstraction of the philosopher, is the real world.

One of the greatest joys of my life as a theologian is the awareness of my closeness to people, not just those of a particular class or culture, but to people of a dozen different countries, with special bonds of closeness to some intimate God-given friends. At the core of my understanding of moral theology is the conviction that nobody grows alone; people need people; we are what our relationships enable us to be. If I have a particular understanding of theology, it is thanks to what I have learned from the masters of the subject through the centuries, but this is deepened and coloured by my own experience of life, enabling me to be 'happy in my own skin', shaped and matured by the familial, cultural, social and historical influences that I recognise as God's gifts, and all of this totally focused on my commitment to Jesus.

Early Years

My life story is fairly simple. I was born in 1927 and grew up in Mullingar, then a provincial town of about five-thousand people. Though life was tough in the 1930s and 1940s in Ireland, I enjoyed an uneventful life in a loving and secure family until age fifteen when my father's death in a traffic accident and a period of debilitating illness for my mother left me, as the eldest of seven children, the father – and in some ways the mother-figure to my younger siblings. I fought with God during those years because I felt this as a heavy burden that I did not deserve, but I still cycled faithfully to 8 o'clock Mass every morning before going to school. Later, in the monastery, I thanked God for that experience, because it gave me a deep sense of responsibility, but more importantly, some maternal instinct and sensitivity.

I have happy memories of school and was very much at home in the faith-culture of family rosary, daily Mass, May devotions, Blessed Sacrament processions and catechism classes. In spite of the limitations of the period, I received a good grounding in knowledge of the faith. I recall being asked at ten years of age in the examination before confirmation: do indulgences give grace?

Hoping to do something worthwhile with my life, I thought of religious life (not diocesan priesthood). As a young teenager most of my meagre pocket money was spent on lives of the saints (Francis Xavier, Dominic, Francis, John of the Cross, Thérèse of Lisieux etc.) and the much-loved books *The Imitation of Christ* and *The Introduction to the Devout Life of St Francis de Sales*. For a time I thought of the Cistercians and cycled eighty miles to spend a weekend in their monastery. I was tempted towards a mission to lepers in Africa. But the Marist preacher of a school retreat persuaded me that my place was with the Society of Mary. I was accepted in 1945. After a year of philosophy in Dublin and my novitiate or spiritual year in the south of England, I was sent to Rome, where I did four years of philosophy and four of theology (all in Latin). I completed the course in 1955 with a Licentiate in Theology and a Doctorate in Philosophy (thesis: *The Eternal Objects in the Philosophy of Aquinas and of Alfred North Whitehead*). My studies were at the Angelicum university and my first year there (1947) overlapped with the second or last year of Karol Wojtyla. When I met him later as Pope John Paul II at a few private Masses in the Vatican, I reminded him of that. A far away look would come into his eyes and he would murmur quietly: 'Ah yes, the good old days, the good old days'.

During my eight years of Roman study, I spent most summers (usually three months) with our students in Italy, France, Spain and Germany. This gave me a fluency in these languages which was very useful in giving retreats and renewal courses from the mid-1950s until the present day, and very particularly when, since the early 1960s, I was invited as moderator, facilitator or translator to about thirty provincial or regional chapters of religious around the world and twenty international general chapters. I began teaching in the Marist house of studies in Dublin in 1955. As superior there from 1961–1967 I was responsible for a farm with ten cows, two-hundred pigs and six-hundred hens, as well as teaching philosophy and theology, with some scripture and liturgy, to the Marist students. In 1970 I joined the staff of the Milltown Institute of Philosophy and Theology, and also taught moral theology for some years in the Mater Dei Institute in Dublin. I spent a total of twenty-five years in Rome, first as a student, then as superior of our international house of studies, and later as secretary general of the Society of Mary from 1983 to 1995.

Theology and Aquinas

I enjoyed Latin in my secondary school and I liked it even more when it was the language in which I did my philosophy and theology. My contact with theology was love at first sight. I can still recall the thrill and the excitement of trying to reach up to the mind of Aquinas. I was captivated by the heights to which his spirit could soar and by his breadth of vision as he reached out to new ideas wherever they were to be found. His concern for truth and his reverence for words left a lasting impression on me, an influence that I still feel and treasure almost half a century later. I could understand why Popes Leo XIII and Pius X should decree that his theology be the standard and only system for all Catholic seminaries. Unfortunately, the classical scholasticism of the middle ages had deteriorated into a narrow and rather wooden system of neo-scholasticism which became totally a-historical, a-cultural and largely cut off from the word of God and the realities of ordinary human life. It seems to survive only in some departments of the Vatican civil service. I was a happy witness to the liberation of theology even before Pope John XXIII was inspired to convoke the Second Vatican Council. I remember the excitement of reading mimeographed copies of the writings of Teilhard de Chardin, and then the heady days and years of the new writers bringing a new dynamism to the intellectual life of the Church. I recall the influential Lenten letter of Cardinal Suhard of Paris in 1947, when he spoke of a new 'springtime of the Church' which would break with the old Catholic triumphalism. Something of what he meant can be seen in the writings of Chenu, Congar, Rahner, de Lubac, Schillebeeckx, Küng, Daniélou and the magnificent Bernard Häring. Much of their thinking found expression in the documents of the Second Vatican Council. What a glorious time that was, with all its promise of a bright and wonderful future. Unfortunately Church leadership prevented the flowering of that beautiful springtime, so that four decades later major problems in theology and church life are still awaiting serious attention.

A basic weakness in the Council discussions was the fact that so many of the bishops were trapped in the neo-scholastic theology that had no awareness of modern historical-critical exegesis or of the transition from classical to historical consciousness. The traditional mindset seemed not to be aware of the fact that there is no word of God in pure unadulterated form, a-temporal, a-historical, a-cultural. God's word comes to us in human words and every human word from the first moment when humans learned to speak is culturally conditioned, reflecting the experience and culture of the speaker. God's will comes to us through the medium of experiences in the world and in the Church. All of these are historically conditioned, hence the need for discernment. I could still venerate the theology of Aquinas, but my understanding of him was enriched by the thinking of Chenu, Congar and Schillebeeckx, who connected his work with the spiritual climate of his time rather than treat it as a supra-temporal unchanging model for all time. This meant broadening theology to include its social, political and cultural context. It follows that theology is not reflection on abstractions (like most of neo-scholasticism), but reflection on a concrete reality in human history, a history that is part of God's plan of salvation. This approach naturally shows up the relativity of any theological system, including dogmatic formulations. It raises serious questions about the Vatican's new category of truths, which are said to be 'definitive' (final, unchangeable) though 'non-infallible', a concept which seems to be the brainchild of just one theologian.

Alienation of the Faithful

Catholics of a certain age can nostalgically recall the joy and hope that filled the Church during the Council, reflecting, as it were, the open, welcoming and very human smile of Pope John XXIII. Many of them have lost that hope and joy, and now feel themselves alienated from the institution that for most of their lives they looked to as their holy mother. They look to their Church to share the good news, to preach the Gospel, to teach the faith. But the impression they get from the Church's own teaching practice is that, without any listening or dialogue, truth can simply be decreed from on high and imposed under obedience, with grave sanctions for disobedience, whereas our human experience is that truth can only be discovered and shared, and teaching means persuading and convincing, not just commanding. In this kind of climate, authority and moral influence can easily degenerate into a concern for power and control.

It was always accepted that clergy (at all levels) are human and would have their share of human weaknesses. To read Church history is a sobering experience. But the sudden revelation of wholesale sexual abuse of children by clergy was a shattering blow to people's faith. They were even more scandalised by the massive and systematic cover-up by Church leaders who too often gave the impression that it was simply a media problem and seemed to have little understanding of or feeling for the tragedy of the victims.

But the large-scale alienation of the faithful was not suddenly triggered off by the scandals. It has been growing for many years because the springtime promised by Vatican II failed to materialise. The Church seems more authoritarian than ever. It is predominantly 'conservative' types that are appointed bishops while the laity have little or no input in the choice. Their role as area managers in the universal Church makes it difficult to see them as successors to the apostles with their individual responsibility in their own dioceses. The laity as a whole feel that they are never consulted on matters that concern them as members of the Church, in spite of their being temples of the Holy Spirit who works powerfully in their Christian faith and in the experience of their lives. Within the laity as a whole, there are special groups who feel excluded from full enjoyment of Church membership – homosexuals, people in second marriages and, to some extent, women. Church leaders invite them to feel at home in God's holy family, but in practice they have all the obligations of being Catholic without the benefits they so long for, like guests invited to the Christmas dinner who are told to wait in the kitchen or hall while the meal is being served to others. Much of my ministry for several decades now has been one of bridge-building and peace-making with these good people, helping them to see the wider picture and assuring them that they are infinitely precious in God's eyes. I am saddened that the Church makes so little effort to examine the faulty theology that is largely responsible for their suffering.

Publications

As a theologian, some of my ministry of the word meant publications, usually in response to requests from editors and publishers. From 1957 until the present I collaborated in nine books, contributed several articles to theological encyclopaedias, recorded tapes on spirituality, wrote many articles and reviewed numerous books. *Has Sin Changed?* (1977) sold over 65,000 copies worldwide and is a talking book for the blind in the United States. Twenty years later, in 1997 *Does Morality Change?* sold 5,000 copies before being republished by Columba Press, Dublin, in 2003. In the early 1980s I was correspondence-counsellor (psychology/spirituality) for the weekly Catholic newspaper *The Universe*, London, when, before computers, I personally replied to several hundred letters a year (three or four of general interest would be published each week). This brought home to me the vast amount of tragic and often silent suffering afflicting God's holy people.

Since the 1960s I have been involved in several dozen television broadcasts on a variety of topics relating to faith and Church from topical issues like marital breakdown, homosexuality and sex abuse, to issues of a supernatual nature like hauntings, possession and exorcism. For over thirty-five years I have had a continuous apostolate to homosexual groups and individuals, and in recent times to some transsexual people. But in the past ten years the saddest cases of all have been the many tragic victims of clerical sex abuse. I cannot help feeling that if some Church leaders, especially in the Vatican, had personal contact with these victims, they might see something of the crucified Jesus to relativise their concern about the public image of his institutional Church. Fears about compensation can distort our priorities and blind us to the call of the Gospel. If I were to describe my most important and most needed ministry in the past few years, I would see it as a pastor to the alienated.

Language is Sacred

Over thirty years ago, after recording a programme for the national television station, I was surprised to hear the producer say with enthusiasm 'I always admire the innocent way you throw your hand grenades on television.' The remark reminded me of a personal conviction that has been part of my theology all during the past fifty years of teaching. It may not be true that the medium is the message, but since God and the things of God are at the heart of our theology, God deserves the very best that we are capable of when we speak about the divine. Language is extremely important. I was hugely impressed many years ago when that excellent communicator and extraordinary witness to the faith, Hans Küng, expressed this same thought. He explained that before his texts were sent to the publisher, they were read aloud to his friend in the German faculty, or the friend would read them aloud to him, so that they could be evaluated as spoken and heard. It was very important that the ideas not only *be* good, but that they should also *sound* good, not as a publicity stunt, but out of reverence for God. It is an ideal that I have always had in mind.

Finally, in all my efforts at communicating theology, I have tried to speak the truth in love. The Second Vatican Council had no hesitation in reminding us that, to be faithful to the gospel, the Church itself is always in need of purification (*Ecclesia semper purificanda*). It is a real disloyalty to the Church, to truth and to God to pretend otherwise. I praise and thank God for all of my past, for life, love, family and friends, and especially for the great gift of Catholic faith and seventy-eight gracious and grace-filled years of life in the Catholic Church which I so passionately love – warts and all!

6.

Biography and Theology: Contexts and Changes

Seán Freyne

Where to begin? The invitation to contribute to this collection could become either an occasion for narcissism or an opportunity to explore the hidden recesses of the self that are rarely, if ever, visited! I have set myself a more modest goal, namely, to map out the changes in focus, methods and perspective that have, at least in retrospect, become evident in my own theological development. My professional life has brought me to very different locations, with different audiences providing the challenge to respond to their questions and their concerns in many different ways. Theology is not, or at least in my opinion should not be, an exercise in providing ready-made answers to fit any and every occasion. It is, rather, an exercise of exploration in the faith that is always provisional and in constant need of revision as we strive for more adequate answers to the pressing questions that confront all of us – questions that are personal, social and cosmic.

If theology is faith seeking an adequate understanding, it is important to acknowledge at the outset my debt to those who introduced me to and aided my first faltering steps in a faith to which I remain deeply attached – immediate family and relations, especially my mother and sister, devout west of Ireland neighbours with their love for Mary and the Mass, and teachers, both lay and clerical. The untimely and sudden death of my father, which as a four-year-old I experienced first hand, left a deep impression on me as well as creating a great sense of loss. It also made me a somewhat introverted and anxious young person, a disposition that I only gradually overcame through success on the sporting field during my teenage years. How such an adolescence might be seen to have influenced my theological development later in life is a moot point, about which it seems idle to speculate now, since any suggestion would inevitably involve some element of projection.

My first introduction to the formal study of theology was disappointing, to put it mildly. In the seminaries of the 1950s we were given all the answers to questions that had never occurred to us, but had been thought up and handed down by dry, scholastic minds for centuries. Rote memory rather than theological imagination was the essential requisite for such an education.

This type of study was so utterly different from that which had been fostered by my primary degree in Ancient Classics that I was often tempted to abandon the whole project. Athens and Jerusalem rarely encountered each other in this seminary theology and yet, ironically, the fact that I was proficient in Greek and Latin was the reason for my being chosen to do Biblical Studies in Rome, or at least so I was informed at the time.

My stay in Rome coincided with the first three sessions of the Second Vatican Council and the whole atmosphere in Church and theology suddenly underwent a dramatic change. It was as though a time-bomb was waiting to go off and suddenly John XXIII had pressed the button. It is not possible to describe here the sense of excitement, exploration and debate that was generated as bishops and theologians gathered in Rome from the four corners of the globe. If the Holy Spirit was directing the Council's proceedings she was speaking in many different tongues and with many different agendas. The sense of intrigue, the expectation surrounding the daily press conferences, the rumours and counter-rumours that coursed throughout the city ensured that there were many stimuli for those who were interested in such games. Yet, despite that all too human side of the Council, our theological education was no longer confined to the halls of academia. It was a thrilling time to be in Rome.

I was fortunate to have been living at San Colombano, the study house of the Irish Columban Fathers. There I was exposed to a very different breed of bishop to those housed under the watchful eye of John Charles McQuaid in the Irish College. Not that the Columban bishops were all radicals, but having been exposed to the very different worlds of China, Japan, Korea and the Philippines, they had each to rethink their own approach to mission while reconciling this uneasily with the Tridentine theology they had learned in the seminary. It was my first and most influential lesson on enculturation as the primary task of theological reflection. It corresponded uncannily to what I was hearing about the Bible in my lectures at the Biblical Institute: Israel's emergence as a people had to be understood in the context of developments in the late Bronze Age within the Fertile Crescent. Its literature as expressed in the Bible was the product of that environment. Even the very notion of the covenant as expressive of Yahweh's election should be understood against the background of Ancient Near Eastern vassal treaties as these could be documented from Mesopotamian texts that were 1,000 years older than the earliest parts of the Hebrew Bible. So much for the timeless truths of my seminary theology! Yet, far from disturbing my simple faith, these insights were liberating. To this day I am convinced that a culturally sensitive interpretation of the Bible (both Old and New Testaments, and indeed of all later theological pronouncements) is demanded by the central declaration of Christian faith: 'The Word became flesh and pitched his tent in our midst' (Jn 1:14). All our words, not least our talking about God, are human constructs, not a message dictated from on high.

Much of early Christian theology was fashioned in the maelstrom of missionary praxis, as Paul's letters so graphically demonstrate. My first appointment was to the Columban seminary in Navan where I was confronted with the task of helping to prepare intelligent and idealistic young Irishmen for the tasks ahead, tasks that called for very different skills to those that previous generations of Irish missionaries had acquired. Those were turbulent times for the Irish missionary movement. The word from the front was that new trends in mission to do with faith formation, social development and the acknowledgement of indigenous cultures were beginning to manifest themselves. Yet for those schooled in the theology of 'outside the church there is no salvation' such new emphases were tantamount to a betrayal of what they believed to be the central task of their missionary endeavours. This was a view that I myself would have shared as late as 1960, on the basis of the then reigning opinion about the necessity of the church for salvation, as this continued to be propagated in Maynooth.

Yet the greater the awareness of indigenous cultures, the more it became obvious that the Bible, with its rich storehouse of images, stories, proverbs, myths and legends, was much more in tune with the Eastern mind than were the philosophical categories of Aristotle or Aquinas. At the same time liberation theology had begun to raise its voice in Latin America as 'base communities' were engaged in a critical reading from their experience of marginality of the Gospel story about Jesus and his concern for the poor. It was only when I joined the editorial board of the journal *Concilium* in 1984 and had the privilege of working with such prophetic scholars as Gustavo Gutierrez, Leonardo Boff, Jon Sobrino and Aloysius Pieris that I was forced to see how such 'ideological' readings of the Bible could be integrated, and indeed enriched by the historical–critical method that I had learned at the Biblical Institute and which I had personally experienced as liberating. Yet the Dalgan Park students of the late 1960s were posing these questions to me, based on what they were hearing from their confrères in Peru, Chile and a little later, the Philippines.

By contrast, the Maynooth students of the early 1970s had much less exposure to such questions when I joined the staff there in 1969. The heavy episcopal control of the situation in the national seminary made it difficult to raise any of these issues publicly. On one occasion I was hauled over the coals by a bishop-visitor because of a rather innocuous reflection on the gospel reading for the day which he overheard as he was making his morning meditation in the side-chapel! 'Keep your theological ideas for the pages of foreign journals; all I want is pastoral priests', was the advice of my own Ordinary when I complained about such interference.

In 1972 I had my first meeting with Professor Martin Hengel at the Institutum Judaicum of the University of Tübingen to discuss my project of bringing together perspectives from both Biblical Studies and Classical Antiquity for the study of the New Testament. He suddenly sprung to his feet and declared that before we got to the New Testament we badly needed a study of Galilee in the Hellenistic and Roman periods, in order to assess the degree to which Greek culture might have influenced even Jesus himself. I did not know then that Hengel was one of those German theologians who were seeking to redress the anti-Semitic strand of German academic scholarship that went back to the nineteenth century, climaxing in the claim that since Galilee was pagan, Jesus was not a Jew. Nor had I any sense at the time that his suggestion to study Galilee would lead to a life-time of engagement with the region, opening up a number of theological as well as purely historical issues of ongoing significance for Christian faith – the possibilities of Jewish–Christian dialogue (since Galilee was the home of both religions) and the Hellenisation of Christianity, to name but two.

Foremost among such issues, however, is the renewed interest in the historical Jesus and the ways in which his social, religious and cultural environment might have influenced his understanding of the kingdom of God and his own role with regard to it. Much has changed in discussions about Jesus since then. One of my earliest contributions to the Irish Theological Association was for a symposium dealing with the human knowledge of Jesus. Even though my ideas had been prompted by an important article from the great Karl Rahner, I was severely criticised by an eminent Irish theologian of the day for suggesting that when Jesus was declared Son of God at his baptism this should be understood as a designation of his messianic status rather than an affirmation of his divinity, as later declared in church councils.

In the interim even the messianic status of Jesus has slipped off the scholarly radar, in favour of various other roles, more social than religious. The modern recovery of what Johann Baptist Metz has described as 'the Synoptic Jesus' (as distinct from the heavenly, Johannine one) can be attributed in large part to the influence of liberation theology with its insistence on salvation on earth, as in heaven, but it is also a result of the secularisation of the discipline, especially in the United States. While my studies of Galilee over the years have taken me on various detours into social, economic and cultural issues, particularly in dialogue with modern archaeological approaches to the region, I have always insisted that Jesus was first and foremost deeply embedded in his own religious tradition. His vision was drawn from that rich heritage of prophetic justice for all and respect for the earth as part of God's creation. Ironically, recent discoveries from the Dead Sea Scrolls show that the issue of the Messiah's role was a very live one in the circles that produced the scrolls, circles that were not far removed from John the Baptist and Jesus also. For me the theological importance of Jesus' Galilean experience is that of 'the scandal of particularity', as Edward Schillebeeckx has described the circumstances of his human life and history.

From a Christian perspective, Jesus' concerns with his own place give meaning to every place; all theology, like all politics, is local, according to the Christian story.

It was during my time in Tübingen that I eventually decided to resign formally from the priesthood and marry Gail Grossman, an Australian whom I had met several years previously and with whom I wished to share the rest of my life. This was a difficult and painful decision, but one that I knew I had to take if I was to be true to myself. For me the clerical world was too constricting and I had become disillusioned with the paltry attempts at reform in the Irish Church. But to say that that was my sole or indeed my primary reason for resigning from the priesthood would be an unworthy rationalisation of something far more basic: I had fallen in love and craved for the intimacy and human support of somebody who loved me unconditionally and had been patient with my uncertainty and vacillation. Once the decision was taken and I had resigned from my Maynooth post I experienced a great sense of freedom, inner peace and excitement at the prospect of making a life together and, God willing, having a family.

This was a momentous change in my personal circumstances and, in the mid-1970s, these were uncharted waters. Would it be possible to continue with theology? How might I begin to retrain myself for life in 'the real' world? 'To dig I am not able, to beg I am ashamed' (Lk 16:3) echoed in my ears more than once as numerous job applications were either ignored or rejected. By a happy set of circumstances I was eventually offered a post at Loyola University, New Orleans, despite the ban on former priests teaching in Catholic Colleges as a condition for the dispensation from celibacy. New Orleans has a special affection in my memories, since it was there that we were able to begin a new life and there our first daughter, Bridget, was born. Sarah, our second daughter, was born in Dublin four years later. The theological enterprise looks very different and the priorities shift once the responsibility and opportunity of parenthood present themselves. Both have learned a strong sense of their own identity as young, independent-minded women from Gail's feminist concerns and studies, while my de-patriarchalisation in life and in theology has continued apace!

Theologically speaking, the changed situation from seminary teaching could not have been more striking. Here were young American college students who had to take courses in theology and philosophy in order to graduate, and many of them had little background, and some even less interest, in the subject matter. Instead of following a set programme one had to tailor courses to the general aims of the Arts curriculum, sometimes actually team-teaching with people from other areas. It was a challenge to one's creative imagination, but one that in retrospect turned out to be a real benefit for my subsequent career. There were new stirrings in the field of Biblical studies at the time and my first meeting of the Society of Biblical Literature was an eye-opener. New methods were in the air – the use of the social sciences, structuralist approaches to texts and, a little later on, feminist readings of the Bible were all hot topics. Many of these approaches, though highly experimental, provided a contemporary key to the Bible that was attractive to students who had little philosophical or theological background, but who found the Bible highly congenial to their own spiritual needs.

More than twenty years later I found myself reverting to some of these approaches when confronted with young Irish students within the Arts curriculum at Trinity College. The move to Trinity was as exciting as it was unexpected. To develop Ireland's first non-denominational School of Theology within an Arts programme was a new challenge, one that both the American experience and a brief appointment at the Department of Religions in Queensland University, Brisbane, had prepared me for in ways that I did not suspect, until the situation presented itself. The single biggest difference of the university as distinct from the seminary context is the demand to keep abreast of one's subject in publishing as well as in teaching. International peer review is the order of the day, but I have found the stimulus of working in an environment where research is not merely encouraged but expected to be highly invigorating.

Like most other areas of Irish life, the universities here are going through a period of rapid change and it is by no means clear what the future of theology will be in the new Ireland and the new university. The present emphasis on science might appear to downgrade all the Humanities, making it all the more important for the universities to be reminded that they are educating for a society and not just an economy. 'Going forward', as the current cliché puts it, a broad curriculum, which should include the study of religion as part of human culture, will have an important role to play in maintaining respect for and understanding of the rich heritage that is currently in danger of being dismissed in the headlong rush for progress. In my experience many scientists are deeply struck by the mystery and beauty of the world, the more intimately they become acquainted with its intricate and delicate design at both the macro and the micro levels. No doubt, theological formation for church ministry, whatever forms that will take, must continue, but as practitioners of a discipline within the Humanities, theologians have a responsibility to maintain the highest academic standards if they are to claim their right to contribute to the public discourse within society at large to which their discipline has so much to contribute.

The pilgrimage of life continues and one is never sure when the great call may come. A recent illness, from which, thankfully, I have made a complete recovery, was a reminder of one's mortality and emphasises the significance of the present moment. My understanding of the faith that I received is today deeply informed by the Biblical sense of the Divine as active, real, but mysteriously present in every aspect of the world and of life. Long ago that God refused to give his name to Moses at the burning bush, but instead made a promise that 'he would be with' Israel on the desert journey. Jesus, the Jewish Galilean, is for me the guarantor of that pledge.

7.

A Passion for Faith

Michael Paul Gallagher

If I ask myself when and where a passion for theology first awoke in me, the answer is clear: in the early sixties, in Caen, a Norman city in the north of France. I had finished a degree in Dublin in English and French literature and was awarded a French government grant for a year in Caen. There in 1961, just as the whole Catholic Church was preparing for the melting pot of Vatican II, the religion of my upbringing was exposed to the very different world of France.

I had grown up in a small village called Collooney in Co. Sligo, had been sent at the age of twelve to a Jesuit boarding school (Clongowes Wood College, Co. Kildare), followed by three years at University College, Dublin. The disturbance of moving between those three Irish worlds was nothing in comparison with the impact of France. Religiously I remained pious throughout childhood and adolescence. During my time at university in Dublin I stayed at an Opus Dei hostel, which healthily challenged me to think about faith. I went to Mass frequently, if not quite every day. I also learned that there was such a thing as theology and browsed in some books that were available. I developed an interest in Scripture, both as food for prayer and as a literary text. The Republic of Ireland in those years was a largely unified and Catholic society. Was it so tight and narrow as we tend to portray it in hindsight? I did not experience it that way. Passive and sheltered, perhaps, but not painfully oppressive.

France, however, was something else. At Caen University I encountered a dramatic diversity of views and lifestyles. Even though I was studying in the arts faculty, most of my new French friends were students of science. I met atheists and unchurched Catholics for the first time in large numbers. But an even greater surprise came from meeting young French believers: they were passionately alive in their faith and introduced me to a dynamic Catholic chaplaincy. There were Bible evenings, meditation schools in local monasteries, social awareness events and visits from famous thinkers, including Gabriel Marcel and a Dominican who was either Chenu or Congar (I don't remember exactly). Even in a provincial town like Caen, we experienced something of the rich ferment of French Catholicism that was to have such an impact on Vatican II.

Encounter with Complexities

It was the mixture of the two worlds that awoke me. On the one hand, this new face of Catholicism, thinking, committed and energetically communitarian. On the other hand, my interaction with contemporaries who had little or no time for Christianity or Church. I realised that in fact my Irish upbringing had given me precious roots that I began to appreciate more in this new context. France was giving my faith new intellectual energy and these unbelieving friends were challenging me to spell out the Gospel in another language (in every sense). Late into the night I discussed questions of meaning both with believers and unbelievers. I discovered that I had a gift, especially with unbelieving friends, to change the wavelength from argument to honest and personal exploration. In short I discovered the passion of my life, which was to focus and develop slowly in years ahead – a passion to make sense of God for people today. Rather like Monsieur Jourdain's speaking 'prose', without knowing it I was on the road towards 'fundamental theology'.

The year after my Caen experience I entered the Jesuits. The idea had been there before even at the end of secondary school. If I had joined then, it would have been in a rather world-despising spirit. But now, after France, I entered with new horizons and an intuitive sense of a mission of making faith real in a world of unbelief, a world for which I now had much more feeling and sympathy. After two years of noviceship, I went to Oxford for special studies in Renaissance literature, doing a thesis on rhetoric in the poetry of George Herbert. I still regard him as one of the great spiritual poets in English, much more real than the more exhibitionist John Donne or the pomp of Milton. At Oxford there were different unbelievers, less anguished than the French and somewhat puzzled by my religious commitment (in those days even non-ordained Jesuits went around in Roman collars). When we had seminars on the religious poetry of the seventeenth century, I realised that the contours of inner experience, captured so marvellously in Herbert, spoke to everyone. A more explicitly religious vocabulary seemed to alienate, due no doubt to childhood memories of church. At this stage I knew little of professional theology but my natural preference was for the symbolic realm as a starting point. Hence by the time I came to study theology, I was shaped by several years of immersion in literature. If France gave me a field of pastoral passion, literature gave me a sensibility that was to prove a criterion of relevance. Merely abstract or doctrinal approaches seemed to ignore the battlefield of today's lived sensibility. Theology, if it were going to be fruitful, would have to speak to people imaginatively. Are we not told in two of the Gospels that Jesus never spoke to the crowds except in parables?

Before I arrived at theology studies, another stage of formation gave me more trust in these shy intuitions. I taught literature for a year at University College Dublin and then had a year as a research fellow in Johns Hopkins University,

Baltimore. The year in the old Earlsfort Terrace location was exciting but its main blessing was the chance to meet and listen to a new generation of Irish students. Among them were some who have since become famous as writers or film makers, and whom I got to know well: Jim Sheridan and Neil Jordan were there that year. Later there were many other future writers who studied English at UCD. In 1967 such contact was like living in the future. I remember saying at a large Jesuit gathering that the culture was shifting and that faith could no longer be taken for granted. Shock. Horror. What was this young Jesuit (of twenty-eight) saying? I escaped to America! It was a year of racial riots and Vietnam-related violence, even outside the door of our house. I don't think I was able to integrate this social dimension into my rather personal view of faith. Not yet. That would happen later, as I will explain. In John Hopkins I ran into the early wave of postmodern thinking in literature, with people like Girard, Derrida and Hillis Miller. I did not understand it at the time but it shook my Oxford assumptions. If literature was no longer a serene field grounded in historical and humanist assumptions, would this not apply to theology as well? Baltimore also nourished my feeling for the world of non-belief, especially through friendship with some agnostic students of Jewish background. The common ground remained the world of poetry or imagination, which protected us from fruitless head trips.

From Literature into Theology

With this perhaps unusual background I came to the study of theology in the Milltown Institute in 1969. Looking back now I find it hard to evaluate those three years. Although some of the courses were stimulating and some of the teachers inspiring, much of the material came across as very churchy to me. To use the famous distinction of Pope John XXIII (borrowed in fact from Cardinal Suenens), the focus was almost exclusively *ad intra*, and all my experience had given me an *ad extra* orientation. I recognise that foundations had to be laid, that first-cycle theology needed to initiate us into the great tradition, and that hence the classical approach could not be jettisoned. But my passion for the contemporary struggles of faith would have been better served by another pedagogy. There remained a gap between the official study of theology and religious realities as I perceived them.

In an unusual step I was asked to continue lecturing in literature in the university, on a part-time basis in the afternoons or evenings, right through these years of basic theology. Some of the Milltown professors viewed this with understandable suspicion. For me it offered a double challenge: on the one hand, to perform well in the theology examinations and on the other hand, to continue to observe the impact of an increasingly secular environment. If I ask what remained with me from those first three years of theology, the answer seems clear. I benefited greatly from being able to research and write essays in various fields. From my literary studies I had acquired a certain pleasure and facility in writing, and the gathering of insights on paper allowed me to appropriate theology more than any other approach. Even today I remember what I wrote on themes such as the history of the doctrine of the Trinity, the parallels between secular and scriptural literary criticism, the difference between conscience and the superego or the role of the Paraclete in the Fourth Gospel. That last topic proved strangely relevant when, in 1994, I was sent in a Vatican delegation to have dialogue with a wise and spiritual ayatollah in Iran!

Immediately after that first degree in theology and priestly ordination I returned to a full-time lectureship in modern English literature in University College, Dublin (UCD), and remained in that post for eighteen years (apart from some sabbatical periods). In the mid-1970s my superiors insisted that I should undertake a doctorate in theology. I had already begun to publish some articles on unbelief among the younger generation in Ireland. It seemed a good idea to explore atheism more theologically and this is what I did with a thesis entitled 'Approaches to Unbelief', which I finished in 1979 for Queen's University Belfast. The faculty there was very accommodating about non-residence and I had as my supervisor the kindly Dr James Haire, a leading Presbyterian scholar who had studied under Karl Barth. I was given great freedom and ended up with a broad-ranging thesis of a comparative kind, which involved a year of travel and field work. I examined different models of response to atheism. These included the transformation of official church attitudes during the debates at Vatican II, the 'theology of atheism' developed by Karl Rahner (whom I met as part of my research), the work of the World Council of Churches in this field and the theology behind the pastoral initiatives concerning unbelievers in France and French-speaking Canada. In a final section I compared these paradigms of theology with the portrayal of atheism in imaginative literature, taking as my key example the novels of Australian Nobel laureate Patrick White, who was a kind of contemporary Dostoevsky. It was not the tightest or most academic of theses but it gave me great satisfaction to gather that convergence together. In fact I was the first ever Roman Catholic to receive a doctorate in theology from Queen's.

The Vatican and the Gregorian

Little did I know where all this would lead. It opened the door to some major and unforeseen changes in my life. Right through the eighties, while continuing my university work in literature, I began to reflect much more explicitly on the changing faith situation in Ireland and to publish articles and books in this area. My first book, *Help my Unbelief* (1983), became a mini best-seller due to a last-minute invitation to appear on Ireland's most popular television programme, the 'Late Late Show' – because an intended celebrity had got sick. In this and in other writings, I never felt called to highly specialist work. Instead I chose, rightly or wrongly, to serve a 'middle-brow' or popular market. I looked on myself as a convergence thinker, asked to communicate between worlds.

Out of this increasing commitment to writing, a second and utterly unexpected turning point happened. My books came to the knowledge of some officials in the Vatican and I was sent for! Not, as happens to some people, to be ticked off. Instead I was asked to serve for five years in the Pontifical Council for Dialogue with Non-Believers, which then merged into the Pontifical Council for Culture. The transition to Rome was not easy for me. I was used to a secular university and now found myself in a civil service, with some research functions. Nevertheless the five years were personally fruitful in that they opened new theological horizons, especially concerning culture. It was also an education in the diversity of faith contexts, since the work entailed visits to very different situations – from Ethiopia to Australia, from Slovakia to Iran.

After the 'quinquennium' ended, my Jesuit provincial decided to risk dividing my life between Rome and Ireland, an arrangement that lasted another five years. In Rome I taught fundamental theology for one semester a year at the Gregorian University, being thus drawn more than before into academic theology. In Ireland I was more freelance, with some teaching commitments at Milltown and Maynooth, and a certain freedom to write and research. In those years I published my most academic theological book, or at least the one with most footnotes: *Clashing Symbols: An Introduction to Faith and Culture*. Since the year 2000 I have been full-time at the Gregorian, involved mainly in the 'second cycle' or postgraduate programme at licentiate level. My teaching regularly involves courses on unbelief and culture and I also teach more specialist seminars on Newman, Lonergan, the relationship between theology and imagination and the history of thinking on the act of faith. It is personally most rewarding to teach students from all over the world, many of whom are going back to their own contexts to teach theology in seminaries and catechetical centres.

Contexts and Roads not Travelled

A one-paragraph digression concerning contexts. It sounds Marxist to say that context conditions consciousness. In 1986–1987 I spent a year in Latin America, with the intention of returning there in a few years to teach theology in Paraguay and to help with religious formation there. That year had a major impact on my approach to theology. It showed me that many of my assumptions had been too individualistic. Living with the poor, I saw that unbelief (my constant concern) was more likely a product of a lifestyle than of a set of ideas. The deepening European secularisation seemed less spiritual and more social. Metz was right: it is what happens when the wellsprings of compassion are blocked or locked into the private realm. On my return to Dublin I lived for three years in a flat in Ballymun (then a socially troubled area), commuting each day by bus to University College. The clash of contexts was fruitful. It opened new horizons for my attempts to theologise. However, the hope to go to Paraguay never materialised. I was called to the Vatican instead and I am still in Rome. I don't regret the might-have-been of Latin America, but I do know that it would have pushed me to think along different lines. Teaching in the Gregorian is an excitingly international experience but its model of theology can suffer from dearth of real context. Both faculty and students are richly multicultural but with the risk of lacking roots in any one culture.

At present I am trying to write a book called *Translating the Giants*. The hope is to draw on some of the great figures of theology who have pondered the question of faith, ranging from Aquinas to Newman, and from Tillich to Pierangelo Sequeri (my favourite Italian theologian of today). The emphasis, however, will be on translating, in the sense of making their wisdom available for a non-specialist readership. With my background, as recounted here, that seems to be my calling in theology. Comparing myself with some of my colleagues in the Gregorian, I am not a 'real theologian'. I don't have it in my blood for decades. There are so many areas in which I would fail a first-year examination. Instead, the convergence of my life asks me to stand at various crossroads or frontiers and to reflect on what I find there. In the past I used to blame myself for not being more academically focussed, but then, according to a Buddhist saying, human unhappiness comes from trying to live more than one life at a time.

8.

Theology in the One World

Werner G. Jeanrond

When I was a student at the University of Chicago I was occasionally asked questions such as 'When did you become a Christian?' or 'When did you meet Jesus Christ as your saviour?' My answer must have disappointed my fellow students: 'I have always been a Christian, though not always in the same way'.

I was born in 1955 in Saarbrücken, Saarland's capital city, and grew up just south of it in a village situated immediately at the French border. In fact, the village extends on both sides of the river Saar and from above it looks like one single community. After the Second World War the German speaking Saarland had received a semi-independent status (with an elected parliament and government) under French authority. Hence in my early childhood there was no unnatural border between the two parts of my village, just the river. It took me two minutes to walk to our Roman Catholic parish church and five minutes to the Roman Catholic parish church on the other side of the river. My parish is part of the Trier diocese and the French parish of Metz diocese. Thus, although my family, parish, primary school and upbringing were very Catholic indeed, early on I encountered differences in Roman Catholic worship, expression, piety and lifestyle. While my parish was extremely well structured in the years prior to the Second

Vatican Council – during Sunday and weekday masses children were organised in rows corresponding to their school classes – the French liturgy was different in tone and, at times, showed signs of moderate disorder as far as children and altar boys were concerned. At the earliest opportunity, immediately after my first communion, I became an altar server, a service that required good mastery of Latin prayers and included faithful attendance not only at selected weekday masses, but also at evening prayer, Eucharistic devotion and rosary prayers.

In 1957 the Saarland joined the Federal Republic of Germany politically, and in 1959 economically. That eventually implied the return of customs officers, border police and the establishment of full national sovereignty between the two parishes. Since, however, on both sides of the river we spoke a Germanic dialect and since most families, like my own, had relations in both 'countries', nobody took the new border regime very seriously. Rather, on the whole, life went on as before. However, the Second Vatican Council's decisions for church reform were implemented in a different tact on either side of the river. With regard to the sacrament of reconciliation, for instance, at some point during the late 1960s the Metz diocese allowed absolution for penitents after a communal penitential service on Saturday afternoon, while the Trier authorities continued to prescribe personal confession as a requirement for individual absolution. I still remember vividly how on Saturdays hoards of 'German' sinners walked over the bridge in order to win a full 'French' absolution of their sins. The French customs officers did not stop these heavy German imports.

Also some Protestants lived in my traditionally Roman Catholic village, a number of them refugees from formerly Eastern parts of Germany. Hence my Catholic primary school was flanked by just enough space for two Protestant teachers who in two classrooms had to take care of nine grades of Protestant pupils. Until 1968 there was a large Catholic schoolyard and a tiny Protestant yard with strict confessional segregation between both playgrounds.

Between 1965 and 1973 I commuted to a Gymnasium in Saarbrücken that, once founded as a Protestant Latin school, now was an ordinary state-run secondary school. Here Catholics and Protestants were taught together, separated only twice a week for denominational religious instruction. Hence from the age of ten I was able to make non-Catholic friends. By then I had learned that there were different denominations, but also some variation between different Roman Catholic traditions. And I had already experienced that national borders might be the result of developments that were beyond local control and interest, and that could be ignored by both children and sinners. Moreover, during my school years the Second Vatican Council led to a dramatically increased public interest in theological issues and made us youngsters aware of the fact that even long-standing religious systems could actually change. We welcomed the new and surprising ecumenical initiatives, including the abolishment of the two school yards in my former primary school. These experiences provided, as far as I am aware, the background for my curiosity to further investigate this complex phenomenon of religion. For me theology was closely related to our life at the border, to its denominational features and radical changes. I decided to find out more about the traditions that formed, inspired and divided us. An open climate for discussion in our local parish youth club further wetted my appetite for theology at a time of heavy social turmoil and change and helped me to articulate my questions.

In 1973 I began my studies of Roman Catholic theology and German language and literature, first at the local university in Saarbrücken and then for one year at the University of

Regensburg. Since the Roman Catholic and the Protestant theology department in Saarbrücken were relatively small, students were encouraged to take courses even in the respective other school. During these years I gained a good knowledge of contemporary Catholic and Protestant theology, was introduced to the Jewish-Christian dialogue, to biblical and historical theology and able to hear and meet many of the then read and debated theological voices from the German- and French-speaking world. I understood that theology was intimately linked to the then ongoing renewal of the church. For me theology was a progressive source of ecclesial, intellectual and cultural renewal.

I became more and more interested in questions of hermeneutics and theological methodology and assume, from today's perspective, that this was so because of the obvious need to discuss criteria and norms for critical and self-critical theological thinking in times of renewal and reform. During the 1970s few theology students accepted uncritical appeals to authority. Our increasing discovery of, and disappointment over, the widespread failure of theologians and church leaders to resist the Nazi regime made us very sensitive to questions of authority in church and society. Neither could we students accept easy appeals to biblical authority – having just been introduced to the historical–critical method and its implications in our Bultmann classes. The pluralism of readings and the limitation of human thinking by space, time and language were epistemological conditions not only for the study of literature, but also for theology. The conservative message of the 1968 encyclical against birth control was widely – and, as we know today, wrongly – interpreted as only a momentary backlash orchestrated by soon to be forgotten Vatican conservatives.

When I left the Saarland for Chicago in 1979, I looked forward to widening my theological horizon and to deepening my concerns for theological method, and I should not be disappointed. The two years as a Fulbright student at the University of Chicago Divinity School offered me insights into many aspects of theology, philosophy and literature. Firstly, I encountered excellent and committed teachers who introduced me not only to theology in the English-speaking world, but who also helped me to read, understand and challenge the most significant theological voices of my own European background in a critical and methodologically serious way. Secondly, I learned to grasp the importance of the history of religions and of comparative studies of religion for Christian theology. And thirdly, I received a thorough training in constructive theological and philosophical methodology by teachers such as David Tracy and Paul Ricoeur. My eyes were opened for the requirements of a genuinely global, pluralist and critical theology, a theology fully committed and appropriately equipped to relate to its three publics – church, society and academy.

When in 1981 the dean of students at Chicago drew my attention to a position of lecturer in theology advertised by the newly founded nondenominational School of Hebrew, Biblical and Theological Studies at Trinity College, Dublin, I grasped the possibility of a great personal and professional adventure. Instead of returning to Saarbrücken where a job as university assistant waited for me, I accepted the challenge and moved to Dublin.

At the age of twenty-six I encountered in Ireland not only a rich religious culture with an ancient heritage and age-old divisions, but also a new vision of theology: theology at the service of all, but outside of all church control. Although some of the Catholic piety I met in Dublin reminded me of the French part of my childhood, the conditions for theology at Trinity College were radically different from any Continental European setting. I became part of a small, though highly motivated team of teachers from Anglican,

Roman Catholic and Presbyterian backgrounds and taught students coming from all sorts of religious traditions or none. Our School was part of the larger Arts Humanities Faculty and on the basis of a contractual arrangement with the Church of Ireland it also offered biblical and theological courses to Anglican ordinands.

During my thirteen years in Dublin I could test in praxis what it means to engage with theology's three publics. Not only did we develop a – for the early 1980s – revolutionary curriculum based on an integrated approach to biblical and theological studies and containing mandatory courses in feminist and liberation theologies. We also offered evening courses for interested adults who had to work during the day. And we organised a public lecture series that attracted an increasingly growing audience – a thousand people and more for internationally known speakers such as Gustavo Gutiérrez and Hans Küng. While representatives of the Roman Catholic Church (not only in Ireland) have officially remained sceptical to any theological training outside of their control and planning (though privately some members of the hierarchy have encouraged our School), most of Ireland's leading Christian thinkers were associated with our school either directly as part time teachers or indirectly as conversation partners, examiners or speakers at our evening programmes. Our work illustrated to the academy, to the churches and to society at large that theology was a significant source for renewal and for overcoming old and questionable social, ethnic and denominational boundaries. A free, but committed theology has an enormous potential to help a culture to detect and discuss the promises and ambiguities of its religious traditions and potential. Not surprisingly, the media took a great interest in our work and vision and often involved us directly in their efforts to contribute to a more enlightened society on either side of this divided island.

My interest in the public role of theology made me visit different initiatives of religious renewal in many parts of

Ireland, such as the Christian Renewal Centre in Rostrevor, Northern Ireland. Here I met my future wife Betty, a Swedish Lutheran from Gothenburg, who worked there as a volunteer in order to support reconciliation between Catholics and Protestants. Crossing the border proved once more to be rewarding in more than an intellectual sense.

Working as a theologian in Ireland made me acutely aware of the need for a critical theological hermeneutics. Only a critical, self-critical, pluralist and public approach to the texts and rituals of all religious traditions in Ireland could enable theological discourse to contribute to mutual understanding. Only such a critical and genuinely dialogical approach to otherness – in our belief in God, in our attitudes to our traditions, communities and own selves – could hope to make room for real reflection and change. However, I also experienced the limitations of a public theology: wherever religion is used to support exclusive power structures and ideologies that consider any acknowledgment of otherness and pluralism as a form of surrender, working for a critical theological hermeneutics, will be met by fundamentalist hostility. I found little difference between Protestant and Catholic hostility in this respect. Theology, it seems, is welcome only where a faith, a tradition, a church, an academic discourse and a society genuinely are prepared to reflect upon their most cherished religious convictions and identities. Nevertheless, any manifestation of biblicist or fundamentalist religious convictions and attitudes in church and society could also be seen as a further argument *for* critical theological reflection and not against it.

Working for ten years with colleagues from all over the world on the board of the international theological journal *Concilium* provided me with a challenging experience of global Christianity and the requirements of a global theology. The plurality of responses to Jesus Christ in this world, the encounter of non-Christian religious traditions and their 'theologies' and the study of the process of ongoing globalisation have further increased my commitment to theological method, especially to a critical theology of correlation, where different interpretations of a tradition, religion, church and culture can, in a mutually critical way, be met by the plurality of expressions of Christian praxis and reflection in this world.

In the Ireland of 1981 a free theology was a novum that attracted first a measure of curiosity but then increasing support and enthusiasm, whereas theology in Sweden had been vanishing from public consciousness since the 1970s. When I took up my position as professor in Systematic Theology at Lund University in January 1995 my chair was the only one left in the entire country that had 'theology' in the title. In all other third-level institutions where courses on religion are taught and where research in religious studies and theology is carried out, what once was named 'theology' was now identified as 'Studies in Faiths and Ideologies/Philosophies'. Of course, there are theologians working in Sweden even outside the Faculty at Lund, but they have not been officially identified as such. Two developments have led to this move in Sweden. Since the Reformation Sweden had been a homogeneous Lutheran state with a state Church. When a secularist critique began to hit the established Church and its various ideological instruments in the country, including the two old theological institutions at Lund and Uppsala, theology became identified with the established confession and any critique of the Church implied also a critique of that sort of confessional theology. Moreover, the rise of an objectivist technological mode in many quarters of the academy, supported by an analytical approach to philosophical thinking, led to a radical challenge to any intellectual discourse considered to be less than fully objective. As a result, faith and theology were deemed subjective, if not altogether ridiculous. Theology was considered to be engaged in confessional activity and therefore lacked the necessary objectivity.

The theological faculties, though keeping their name, responded to this change in intellectual climate by subordinating their research perspectives to the new objectifying regime and, at the same time, expected the church itself to carry on with the necessary constructive and normative theological tasks. Hence, universities were concerned with religious studies – objective, unengaged and removed from religious praxis – while the churches were concerned with their own practical theological concerns. The search for a more adequate understanding of the concept of God, the concern for interreligious dialogue and the work for a critical and self-critical theology that could serve all three of its publics had receded from the academic agenda. Who should respond now to the dramatic return of religion to the forefront of social, political and emancipatory sensibilities in all Western countries? Who should contribute a theological perspective to urgent discussions on ethical implications of new technologies as long as normative theological considerations were considered to belong to the private sphere?

However, even if this was not envisaged by the reformers who had relegated theological concerns from the public to the ecclesial and private realm, the dismantling of an old-style confessional theological regime in Sweden had opened anew a space for a different theology, now thoroughly critical and non-denominational. This explains why I have been able to experience in the churches, in the academy and in society at large such a strong interest in a critical theology. A free and constructive theological voice has a lot to contribute even in post-secular Sweden. Understood as a pluralist and public exercise, theology is at the service of all groups in this society and – without wishing to dominate – can contribute to the increasing interest in God, God's self-manifestation in this universe (in Israel, Jesus Christ, the church and other traditions of faith), the understanding of love, hope and faith in our time, the global character of any serious conversation on religion and the multidisciplinary search for always more adequate ways of understanding the network of relations in which every human being lives: my relation to other persons, my relation to nature and the universe, my relation to the divine mystery and its revelation, my relation to the history and future of humankind and my relation to my own emerging self.

Theology is neither faith nor religion; at best it becomes the critical conscience of both faith and religion. Wherever people wish to deepen their faith, challenge their traditions, desire to explore more of God's mystery, long for a better church, relate critically to religious pluralism without falling into relativism, understand their hermeneutical predicament and work for transformative and emancipatory co-operation in this one world, a critical theology is needed. Such theology must be prepared to challenge artificial boundaries and inward-looking identities. It could encourage promising inquiries beyond one's preferred locality, on the other side of the river, so to speak.

9.

Retrieving Woman's Theology

Mary T. Malone

Bearing in mind the oft-repeated assertion that autobiography is part fiction, it is nevertheless a worthwhile challenge to one's memory and integrity to attempt to trace the contours of one's life. When one's theological development is added to the mix, with its combination of the definable and the indefinable, the enterprise becomes even more challenging. This is only one of the reasons why I approach this task with some trepidation. Let me state the most explicit reason in the form of a confession. The fact is that I have never engaged in the formal study of theology. I have not attended even one theology course. I belong to the generation of women to whom this privilege was denied, when the study of theology was almost exclusively geared, in the Roman Catholic tradition, to the exercise of priestly ministry. I do not hesitate, however, to use and accept the designation 'theologian' for reasons that will become obvious.

At the same time, the vagaries of life were such in the 1960s and 1970s of the Canadian Catholic Church where I resided, that, equipped with a doctorate in patristic literature, gained in the classics department of a secular university, I was teaching theology in an ecumenical consortium of theological schools by the early 1970s. My students were an assortment of female and male seminarians from the main Christian traditions, and eventually a whole new generation of young women and men who sought to engage in the study of theology for its own sake.

Each constitutive college had its meagre ration of women professors. I was on the faculty of the Roman Catholic Archdiocesan Seminary, initially as a patristic theologian, but eventually responding to other assorted demands of the post-conciliar context.

It is only as I look back on this concatenation of events that I realise how very odd it all was. At the time, the world seemed to be unfolding as it should and none of us was fully aware of the radical historical newness of the situation. It was in the give and take of this situation that my own theology developed. It was not long before the traditional curriculum of 'seminary' theology was experienced as inadequate by this new generation of students and teachers. The 'theology of the Second Vatican Council' was beginning to make demands and, in a completely fortuitous way, the second wave of the Christian Feminist movement was exercising its own destabilising influence on the lives of students and professors alike. Besides, as both students and scholars arrived from around the world, the strands of liberation theology and its new demands for 'praxis' were added to the mix. As the 'lay' students began to create for themselves new forms of ministry, two streams of theology became apparent – the academic and the pastoral/ministerial.

The exhilaration of this period is almost unimaginable now, but before describing some of this ferment of active theologising, it is appropriate to take a step back to look at the ingredients that I brought to this historical ecclesial moment. From a sheltered Catholic childhood in a north County Wexford village (where the phrase 'down the Gorey road' sketched the horizons of possibility), I had proceeded through National School and convent boarding school to become a member of a religious community in a fairly seamless journey. I am not now able to unearth the full motivation for the choice of religious life, but somewhere along the line I had been told that it was perfectly legitimate to spend my whole life doing nothing but search for God and a thirst had been awakened. One other childhood circumstance has also been a constant shaper of my theological journey. In the upper half of the family I was the lone girl among three brothers. We were close in age and one form of sibling rivalry seemed, in my memory, to focus on the constant taunt that I could not name one great woman artist, writer, scientist or composer. The nagging question: 'Where are the women?' combined with the thirst for God has formed the backdrop of my personal and professional theological journey.

After my initial degree at University College, Dublin (UCD), I eventually completed my doctoral studies in the University of Toronto. The focus of my thesis on Christian attitudes to women as illustrated in Latin and Greek patristic writing to the end of the sixth century aptly united my two concerns: women and the search for God. This work, directed by a professed atheist, who was in no way unsympathetic to my research, entailed a study of women in the scriptures and the perusal of much of the patristic corpus. My research pre-dated most of the eventual rich resources of feminist exegesis, feminist history and feminist theology, and so, in many ways, I was left to my own resources. Some knowledge of biblical, patristic, conciliar and 'magisterial' theology was obviously essential to this research and I conducted my own theological education on a 'need to know' basis. It was this immersion in biblical and patristic literature that provided a broad and lasting basis for my theology. The question of women in the Christian tradition was central to much of patristic anthropology, Christology, trinitarian theology and the theology of grace and sin. The role of Mary, mother of Jesus, was a kind of essential backdrop to much of this teaching. These issues remain central to my own theological search. It is, of course, not an accident that these same theological questions inform the contemporary tasks of feminist theology.

My eventual departure from my religious community in the mid 1970s, after seventeen years, had no immediate consequences for my theological journey, nor in fact for my position as a teacher. My research circled around the historical sources for the contribution of women to the Christian theological tradition, but the bulk of my teaching was in the department of history. One's public acceptance of the designation as 'feminist' entailed, however, a multi-disciplinary approach to the whole theological realm. It was seen as the task of the very few women professors to be both the instigators and executors of the many curricular changes. It was also expected that the women on the faculty would provide a kind of pastoral oversight for women and men struggling with new theological issues arising from challenges to 'generic' theology by what was often dismissively termed as 'special interest' theologies. My early explorations in feminist theology and feminist history-making were conducted in a context where there were, as yet, no blue-prints and no agreed methodologies. My 'need-to-know' theological method was encountering new challenges. The well-known feminist exegetes and scholars were just beginning to publish, and the demands of time and work meant that it was only by degrees that the women professors learned the art of networking and shared scholarship. We also had to develop the kind of institutional antennae that determined the depth and extent of our theological challenges and the consequences for our own integrity and for our ongoing employability.

The task of communicating this theology became the main focus of the feminist theologian. The traditional *fides quaerens intellectum* meant little, if theology did not communicate meaning. Whereas, for seminarians, it may have been a question of mastering [sic] a certain curriculum toward the goal of ordination, this was not the case for the new breed of 'lay' theological students. These young women and men (eventually mostly women) expected theology to have reference to their lives of faith, parenting, work and active ministry. A new and exciting theology of ministry in the local church as well as the broader theological demands of the global Christian reality meant that theological boundaries were always shifting. Women theologians often seemed to be caught in a theological vortex comprising student demands, personal scholarly goals and ecclesiastical decrees.

In the midst of the excitement of these events, which probably recurred on every theological campus to some degree, my own theological journey was running into difficulties. Recently, Jürgen Moltmann, commenting on his theological experiences in the United States, remarked that, not being black, female or oppressed, black theology, feminist theology and liberation theology were not the central foci of his life.[1] He professed himself happy to return to what was implied as 'real' theology. I was in a similar dilemma but in a different context, and my difficulty was well expressed in the ancient Christian formula of *lex orandi lex credendi*. The total fabric of my Christian life seemed to be unravelling. Alongside my teaching, as was common with many women professors, I had been called to engage in various kinds of extra-curricular activity – extra-curricular, that is, to the university, but not to the task of theology. I was involved at many levels of the total Archdiocesan ministerial effort. This included coordination of catechetical and liturgical endeavours, the development of faith – education programmes for teachers, travelling the lecture circuit as part of new episcopal adult education initiatives and eventually the organisation of the Rite of Christian Initiation of Adults, not to mention a multitude of ecumenical endeavours. Besides, in the new attempted spirit of inclusivism, every committee and every task needed a woman representative. At the same time, Christian women were beginning to organise around the issues of spirituality and women's ecclesiastical roles. At the core of these lurked the question of ordination. Earlier, as a result of my doctoral research, which included the translation and analysis of early church documents on women's diaconate, I had been part of an activist group seeking the restoration of the diaconate for women today. The initial naiveté which inspired such endeavours soon gave way to a much more realistic sense of the intransigence of official ecclesiastical attitudes.

By the end of the 1970s, especially after the publication of *Inter Insigniores,* women's groups reorganised themselves. Instead of directing their efforts towards making space within traditional church structures, some Christian women made the choice of acting as church and developing their own spirituality and theology, in a more woman-centered way. It was in this context that questions of language, liturgy and prayer began to take centre stage: *lex orandi, lex credendi.* For myself, the language and symbolism of prayer and liturgy became a real obstacle, not only to my own theological and spiritual journey, but essentially to my integrity as a woman Christian teacher. It was no longer a question of including women as a gesture of theological courtesy, but, in a direct antithesis to the choice of Jürgen Moltmann, I discovered, this time in the depths of my being, that traditional generic theology, the supposedly 'real' theology to which he could turn in comfort as a male Christian, was no longer adequate for me. This theology had been created by men, lived in by men, ritualised by men, explicated by men, taught by men and seemed to provide male *intellectum* for the experience of male *fides*. It was a theology *prescribed* for women who were seen either as peripheral to or subsumed in the main theological tradition.

This was not just a challenge for me at an intellectual level, but much more intensely at the level of *orandi,* of prayer, both communal and personal. The ongoing and brilliant researches of feminist exegetes and theologians provided much understanding and insight at an intellectual level. In the actual doing of theology and in the exercise of ministry, women were attempting, often against great odds, to act on a perceived call to full participation in the concrete and pastoral life of the churches. From these women came volumes of practical and inspirational contributions in the development of women's ritual, music, spirituality and reflection on new experiences of ministry in family and school, on the streets and in prisons, in hospitals and institutions of all kinds.

In my own faith and theological journey, something essential was still missing and I pin-pointed it in my childhood question: 'Where are the women?' I needed to know the women of the Christian tradition, what they had believed and thought about their faith lives. I needed to know how they had prayed. I needed to know if there had been a women's theological tradition. I needed to access women's theological thought on the processes of birth and death, of caring for children and burying children, on preaching and teaching and working, on living and loving, on power and powerlessness. I needed to know what it was like to be a woman Christian in the imperial Christianity of the fourth century as well as the utterly bewildering Christianity of the plague-ridden fourteenth century. I needed to know, not only that women in their thousands had been burned as witches and heretics, but who these women were and what Christianity might possibly have meant to them. And I needed to know all of this, and so much more, in their own words. As a historian, I knew well that most of this was virtually inaccessible today, but also that such concerns had not been the instigating questions of most preceding history-making. So the search had to begin again, as if nothing had yet been discovered. In my own mind I called this 'WomanChristianity'. It was not a question of disproving or delegitimising 'generic' theology. This theology had served the churches well. I myself had revelled in its patristic 'golden age' and the varied theological high points of Christian history. But for me this theology was now but a partial *intellectum,* a partial entry point to the full meaning of Christianity. My search for 'WomanChristianity' was an attempt to provide a continuous historical basis for today's feminist theology. I wanted to discover a continuous and consecutive narrative of women's Christian lives, not just a series of vignettes fitting into the 'main' story.

One enormously rich resource for this endeavour is, of course, the corpus of medieval women's mystical writing, which alone could challenge generic theology at every level, from the naming of God to the living out of the mystical life in the public exercise of compassion. Here at last I felt at home in a way that had not been possible in my delvings into other forms of theology. This was not a naïve attempt to translate medieval women's mystical theology into the twenty-first century, but a core spiritual response to theological insights that were altogether new in their total impact. For once, *lex orandi* seemed to be intimately related to the *lex credendi*. It is impossible to sum up the theological insights of women mystics in this short paper, but a brief summary of their most relevant teachings will illustrate my point.

First of all these women had to reclaim the fullness of the human condition from which all previous (and subsequent) theology excluded them. It was in and through the humanity of Jesus that they learned to be female human beings. Instead of the prescribed experience of being at a greater distance from God than males, they set out on a journey towards intimacy and direct access to a God who was discovered not only in the traditional mystical 'Book of Creation' and 'Book of the Scriptures', but also in the radically new 'Book of Experience'. Almost without exception, these women experienced the need to address their God in a gendered way and their writings illustrate a glorious confusion in their naming of God. Of one thing they were absolutely sure – their God could not be contained in traditional or indeed any kind of formula. The experience of intimacy with God seemed to replace the traditional (and contemporary magisterial) insistence on self-sacrifice as being the more appropriate model for women. Besides, the mystical journey was, for them, a democratic endeavour and all were invited to pursue this path. This not only freed women to search for God, but freed God to act and be present in the most unexpected ways. The end result of this mystical journey was not a removal from the world but a launching into the world in the public exercise of compassion. In a most revealing way, these women experienced no dichotomy between the traditionally understood active and contemplative dimensions of life.

It is clear that, hidden in this mystical experience, is a rewriting of traditional approaches to God, Christ, grace, anthropology and ethics. It is a strain of Christian theology that bubbles up every now and then in times of disruption and newness. Such a time was the immediate post-conciliar period, where alternative possibilities seemed to present themselves. The theological task before me, as I understand it myself – there are not many dialogue partners on this theological road – is to continue to explore the theological insights of the other half of the Christian community.

I have no doubt that the road forward in theological development, in Ireland as elsewhere, is along the path of community theology. In many ways, this is theology on a 'need to know' basis. It is theology that attempts in today's context that old task of *fides quaerens intellectum*. What is needed is not a replaying of 'seminary' theology. Today's theology has to begin from listening to the faith questions of this generation of adults. I do not know to what extent theological curricula are constructed on the basis of the questions of the participants, but the dialogue between 'generic' theology and today's theological questioning is inevitable. My own theology is rooted in the necessity of including the 'Book of Experience', and especially of women's experience, both historical and contemporary, in the development of this new theology. A good starting point might be a retracing of the ancient path of *mystagogy*. Those newly baptised in the Christian community were invited to 'name what they had come to know' along their journey of initiation. What an explosion of new energy this practice of mystagogy might introduce into the Irish church. A good place to begin might be the exploration of the meaning of the 'God' in whom ninety percent of the population professes belief.

Notes

1. 'A Lived Theology,' in Darren C. Marks (ed.), *Shaping a Theological Mind: Theological Context and Methodology* (Aldershot: Ashgate, 2002) 87-95.

10.

On Trying to be a Theologian

John D'Arcy May

The title 'theologian', I have always felt, is not something one can simply claim for oneself, even if one holds degrees in the subject. Like the title 'poet', it is properly conferred on those who have shown evidence, not just of historical, philological or philosophical learning, but of an ability to evoke and clothe in language the things of God. Like poetry, theology grows out of life and demands a certain diction, easily recognised but difficult to achieve, which makes statements about ultimate meaning convincing. The theologian is of course supported by, indeed is the voice of, an ecclesial community, however structured, to which he or she is responsible. But the indispensable element of personal story in theology makes biography its natural medium.

I studied theology under the *ancien régime* of a pre-conciliar Roman Catholic missionary order: three years of scholastic philosophy, mixed with a dash of modern philosophy, natural sciences and – incongruously – Old Testament, followed by four years of theology. I was actually looking forward to starting theology, although it meant renouncing my first love, English literature, because it offered the prospect of further study of scripture as John XXIII exposed a stultified tradition to the wind of the Spirit at the Second Vatican Council. I will never forget the shock of arriving back in my native Melbourne in 1964 to find theology still being taught out of Latin textbooks which strained even our lecturers' credulity; works by Protestant authors marked 'P' and only to be consulted – not read! – with special permission; and anything that was on the Index of Forbidden Books – that is to say, the key works of the Enlightenment and modernity – locked away from curious students in a glass bookcase (though to add to the general air of schizophrenia, several of my fellow-students had been studying the same works at university in Canberra). The current attack on 'modernity' by the advocates of 'postmodernity' is therefore something I feel I can stand aside from, because I had to find my own way to acknowledging diversity and 'otherness'. It was as if we had been placed in a time capsule which shot us back to the ancient world, then, after a quick tour of the Patristic period, fast-forwarded us to the high Middle Ages for an extended stay, after which we made the acquaintance of the forces of reaction in eighteenth and nineteenth century France. I found Newman's *Grammar of Assent* important as an antidote to desiccated scholasticism and when I mentioned to a highly intelligent fellow student that I was reading Mircea Eliade's *Patterns in Comparative Religion* with enthusiasm, he replied: 'What's that got to do with theology?' An instinctive humanism, reinforced by the priests who gave me such a generous secondary education, refused to succumb completely to piety and clericalism.

All this was happening in the sectarian atmosphere of 1950s and 1960s Australia, when Catholics were still living in a virtual intellectual ghetto and a group of staunch churchmen had left the Australian Labor Party over anti-Communism. The granting of state aid to Catholic schools had released torrents of vitriol, and a book appeared with the title *Catholics in the Free Society*, implying that this was a major problem for a democracy. Ecumenism was just becoming respectable and I was deeply moved by the first ecumenical service ever held in the seminary chapel, the first time I had ever been present while Protestants prayed. Perhaps even more significantly, the scandal of Australia's involvement in the Vietnam War without any democratic process shocked all of us into the realisation that we were not just an outpost of empire but neighbours of the vast populations of Asia and the more vulnerable ones of Aboriginal Australia and the Pacific Islands. Studying with a missionary order had already made this more vivid; we were aware of missionaries working in the Philippines and Japan, and we had heard of places like Merauke, Rabaul and the Trobriand Islands. The idea was forming in my mind that, instead of becoming a missionary or a school teacher, I should study an Asian language and culture in order to learn what the world of one of the great religions felt like from the inside. If I was clear about one thing, it was that I did not want to be sent to Rome for further study.

And, of course, Rome it was: these were not yet the days when religious entered into a 'process of discernment' in order to discover that their will was God's will. My Asian proposals were regarded as unworkable, which they probably were (though since then some of the people who so advised me have been doing precisely what I envisaged in China and India). In 1967 it was still rather special to be travelling to Europe and thanks to a sympathetic travel agent I managed brief but unforgettable stopovers in Hong Kong and Delhi, my first overwhelming and scarcely comprehensible encounters with Asia's massive poverty and religious tensions. With Rome, however, first glimpsed in the pink light of dawn from the plane, it was love at first sight. The city's inexhaustible fascination, its layers of history and the vitality of its people, seduced me and made every single day of my two years there interesting – except for the theology. Post-conciliar Rome was in the grip of a crippling uncertainty: how seriously were the reforms really to be taken? Had the Council meant what it said? In moral theology, which I did not have to study, there were intense off-the-record discussions on the relationship between 'nature' and 'person' in the build-up to the expected statement on artificial contraception; in dogmatics, which was prescribed, there was a cautious opening to the ecumenical and the secular. I made the acquaintance of Barth and Gogarten, and I even pulled off the coup of being allowed to write my Licentiate thesis on the novels of Samuel Beckett under the pretext that they represented 'secularisation', a notion that would have made Beckett shake his head in despair.

When 'the encyclical' *Humanae Vitae*, finally appeared in the famous summer of '68, I had just arrived in London for a summer school on modern English literature and I vividly remember reading the text in *The Times* on the way to Stratford, surrounded by politely sceptical-to-cynical American Eng. Lit. majors, to see a performance of *As You Like It*, which seemed strangely contemporary with its drop-outs in the forest and its easy humanism. I remember the discomfort of Bruce Kent as he tried to preach about the encyclical at the university chaplaincy. The realisation dawned on me that of the many important issues raised by the encyclical, the main one was not birth control but authority in the Church. When the opportunity arose to pursue doctoral studies with Walter Kasper in Münster, I seized it with both hands, leaving my beloved Rome with almost inordinate haste in the hope of finally coming to grips with theology in a modern university setting.

Disconcertingly, Kasper waved aside my half-formed notions of doing a doctorate on theological imagination and pointed me in the direction of Church unity, a subject that seemed too ecclesiastical to arouse my interest, but it meant that after his departure for Tübingen a year later I found my intellectual home for the next twelve years (1971–1983) in the Catholic Ecumenical Institute, whose Director, Peter Lengsfeld, was a German professor trying by every means then available – Jungian psychology, sensitivity training, eventually Zen Buddhism – *not* to be like a German professor. Although I had the privilege of attending Karl Rahner's last two semesters before ill health forced him to retire and theological stars like Johann Baptist Metz were at their zenith, I gained most from my colleagues in what the Germans call the university *Mittelbau*, those doing doctoral or post-doctoral work as *Assistenten*, traditionally the lackeys of authoritarian professors but in Lengsfeld's case acknowledged as co-researchers and given teaching responsibilities. These were people steeped in the traditions of the Enlightenment and modernity yet passionate about theology – just what I was looking for. Because I was English speaking it was assumed that I was an expert in British 'ordinary language' philosophy and linguistic analysis, so as well as plunging into Horkheimer and Adorno, Gadamer and Habermas I had to catch up on J. L. Austin and John Searle. The Institute's research project was to re-conceive ecumenism with the help of the social sciences. In this I became fully engrossed, eventually contributing several chapters to what became known as our 'blue book', *Ökumenische Theologie. Ein Arbeitsbuch* (1980). My own dissertation, which to my dismay I found I had to write in German, was a virtually unreadable attempt to undertake a sociolinguistic analysis of the 'official theology' in the documents of the Second Vatican Council and the World Council of Churches, but it taught me how to tease out the ideologies encoded in the language of institutions and allowed me to breathe the freer theological air of the ecumenical movement.

Up to now this account has seemed rather bookish, and so it is, because I had had the dubious privilege of having nothing to do but study. Now, however, I looked around for something 'real'. I joined a group of Marxist students, but as they did nothing but discuss Marx, I moved on to a group who were trying to teach unruly Spanish and Portuguese *Gastarbeiterkinder* German. In the summer holidays I got work assisting hospital chaplains in London and New York, experiences rich in the discovery of human dignity and diversity. All this time the conviction was ripening that it was as a lay person 'in the world' rather than as an ordained cleric that I could best continue as a theologian. It was a difficult decision, but it has been confirmed by love and marriage many times over. Anything as practical as a job was still over the horizon, though in the event I got a generous university scholarship and Lengsfeld appointed me his *Assistent*.

But theology? Another conviction was forming, or rather re-emerging after the years spent immersed in Reformation, Enlightenment and modernity in Europe: there were still 'the others', the great religions and their counterparts among indigenous peoples. In Münster, especially in the ambience of Metz, all attention was focussed on Latin America, but if I as an Australian was regarded as culturally 'European', surely the Latin Americans were too, whereas in the Asia-Pacific radically different and specifically religious challenges demanded attention. On making tentative enquiries of the Indologists in their small institute above a shoe shop on the Salzstrasse, I found they welcomed anyone who showed an interest in what, in those revolutionary days, was disdainfully regarded as an *Orchideenfach* (a minority 'orchid subject' fit only for the hothouse). I embarked on what was supposed to have been my *Habilitation* or post-doctoral thesis, *Meaning, Consensus and Dialogue in Buddhist–Christian Communication: A Study in the Construction of Meaning* (1984), which had the desirable side effect of earning me a doctorate in History of Religions.

What then? Lacking the resources to travel to Asia, I took to participating in conferences of theologians from Asia, Africa and Latin America at the ecumenical institute of the World Council of Churches in Bossey, near Geneva, at which only a handful of us 'Euro-Americans' looked on while the representatives of the 'young churches' gave vent to their disdain for our pallid rationality and disagreed passionately with one another along lines laid down by their teachers' teachers – Barth, Bultmann, Brunner and the rest. It was exhilarating, and it led to a contact which changed the course of my life, again. Theo Ahrens, then the North Elbian Lutheran Church's liaison officer for the missions in India and Melanesia, was head-hunting for a person who could infuse some theological life into the moribund Melanesian Council of Churches in Papua New Guinea. Would I be interested? Would I!

Because I was to be funded by the Lutheran Church in Bavaria through the Catholic development personnel agency in Cologne, the whole complicated arrangement took two years to set up, providing the German churches with an opportunity for practical ecumenism. After various difficulties in finding affordable accommodation, it was finally settled that I should be based at the ecumenical Melanesian Institute in Goroka, administrative centre of Eastern Highlands Province, and commute to the Council of Churches in the national capital, Port Moresby. This proved extremely advantageous, not only because most parts of the highlands and the north coast can be reached by road from Goroka, but because I was among real experts on the questions of theology and anthropology, Gospel and culture that interested me. Perhaps the most satisfying part of my work, though, was with the Melanesian Association of Theological Schools, which brought together the seminaries and colleges of a wide range of churches, from Nungalinya near Darwin in northern Australia to Kohimarama near Honiara in the Solomon Islands (I think I am still the only person to have visited every member School!). The theoretical concerns that had seemed so important in Europe now seemed somewhat irrelevant and remote. Theology, on the other hand, not being merely theory, was breaking out everywhere in a context where Christian life was vigorous and varied and crying out for reflection.

At the first general meeting of the Melanesian Council of Churches which I attended, the outstanding United Church Moderator, Albert To Burua, a Tolai from East New Britain and a member of the WCC's Central Committee, held up the newly-agreed 'Lima Document', *Baptism, Eucharist and Ministry* (1982) and proclaimed: 'This is the way ahead for us!' I then set about organising a Melanesian study of the document leading to an ecumenical response, which eventually found its place in the volumes edited by the WCC. I also helped the theological colleges found a journal, *The Melanesian Journal of Theology*, which I am pleased to see is still appearing. Things like this I saw as a modest but crucial contribution: helping Melanesians to 'do it their way' in the sense of coming out with their secret thoughts about Christianity and the ecclesial forms in which it had been brought to them, but to 'do it our way' by expressing themselves in print, in English, so that they could be understood and responded to around the Pacific and around the world. There is no way of capturing in a few words the wealth of experience, both human and Christian, and the daily lessons in the elementary human nature we all share, which the four and a half years in Papua and New Guinea (early 1983 to late 1987) brought me. I am eternally grateful to the friends in the University of Frankfurt's *Theologie Interkulturell* programme who importuned me to give the 1988 lecture series, which became *Christus Initiator. Theologie im Pazifik* (1990), because it forced me to distil all these impressions into theology before memory faded.

After all this, Ireland provided another and even more profound culture shock – quite unexpectedly, because I am of Irish descent and this was Europe, after all. But it was a very complicated and troubled corner of Europe in 1987, and I could not believe that such entrenched and antagonistic positions as Nationalism and Unionism could be defended with such full-throated Christian conviction. An invitation to join the Inter-Church Group on Faith and Politics was invaluable: it was an ongoing seminar on the religious roots of the conflict and the potential of the churches to contribute to a solution. It was a truly representative group from north and south, clergy and laity, men and women from most of the Christian traditions, the only one I knew in which people from both 'sides' could crack jokes at one another's expense. This was the closest I came to the 'political theology' I had come to take for granted in Germany and I thought it could lead to a specifically Irish 'liberation theology' with reconciliation, not just confrontation, at its core.

My day job, however, was to be Director of the Irish School of Ecumenics (ISE), at that time a small ecumenical institute backed largely by committed Christians in Ireland and overseas – but not, officially at least, by the churches. ISE offered me from the very beginning the chance to do theology as I think it should be done, indeed must be done, in the times ahead: ecumenically among Christians, in dialogue with the world's other religious traditions and explicitly political, urging ethical and religious perspectives on issues of economic, ethnic and gender justice around the world. The years of teaching the theology of religions, Buddhist–Christian relations and the contributions of the social sciences and the 'primal' religions of indigenous peoples to ecumenical theology have led me to confront aspects of my Christian faith whose traditional formulation I can no longer take for granted. I find my understanding of the mystery of God pared down to the absolute minimum, a transcendence which must be expressed negatively but whose emptiness, like its Buddhist counterpart, is inexhaustible fullness. I tried to formulate something of this in *Transcendence and Violence: The Encounter of Buddhist, Christian and Primal Traditions* (2003). Is this, then, theology? As I promised at the beginning, I'd rather let my readers and students judge!

II.

A Mayo Theologian! God Help Us

Enda McDonagh

Irish Beginnings

In the Ireland of the 1950s one might aim to be ordained a priest but did not set out to be a theologian. Even if one ended up after ordination in post-graduate studies and then with a job teaching theology, such was the culture that one would be reluctant to accept the title theologian. This was illustrated clearly in the comment of the subsequent Bishop of Kildare, Paddy Lennon, during his time at St Patrick's College, Carlow: 'I am not a theologian, I am a teacher of theology'. Although this remark was made in the 1960s, even then Irish ecclesiastical culture and theological practice were changing under the increasing influence of visiting scholars and of Vatican II. The establishment of the Maynooth Union Summer School in the late 1950s gave a public platform to foreign theologians including Louis Bouyer and Charles Davis from France and England, the Germans Bernhard Häring, Joseph Fuchs and Joseph Ratzinger and a host of others such as Raymond Brown from the US, as well as theologians from the UK and Europe. The founding of the Irish Theological Association and the Irish Biblical Association in the late 1960s provided formal indigenous structures for the professionalisation and mutual support of Irish scholars in these fields. Indeed the growing community of Irish theologians and scripture scholars, contemporary and younger, remain a constant positive influence. Such developments may seem old hat now but they had an important influence on many theologians of an earlier generation.

It would be ungracious to ignore the work and influence of still earlier teachers and theologians and of publications like the *Irish Theological Quarterly*, first established in 1909 and re-founded in 1951. Influential journals such as the *Irish Ecclesiastical Record* and *Studies* would not have regarded themselves as primarily theological and neither would their later companions such as *The Furrow* and *Doctrine and Life*. Yet all of these published important theological material in articles and in answers to theological questions from readers. The prestigious American quarterly, *Theological Studies*, frequently commented in its review of current moral theology on such Irish material, particularly on the answers to moral questions in the *Irish Ecclesiastical Record*. Earlier still theologians such as William Walsh, Walter Mac Donald and William Moran, despite or because of their difficulties with some Roman authorities, produced significant work. In scripture too Edward Kissane, Patrick Boylan, Conleth Kearns and others were internationally recognised. So early twentieth century Ireland was not a complete desert, even if theology as a discipline did not rate very highly in Church, university or society. And the six years of theology at Maynooth, from BD through STL to DD, 1951–1957, was not simply narrowly scholastic and provided a substantial grounding in the main disciplines which was often critical and occasionally inspiring. It proved a firm foundation for future theological development.

By the end of that six years a few lasting connections had been made with fellow-students, theological themes, professors and publications. The themes might be given first mention as they continued to be influential, although, by one of these ecclesiastical accidents, they did not figure in my original teaching mandate of 1958 to teach fundamental moral theology, in the chair vacated by William (later Cardinal) Conway when he became Auxiliary Bishop of Armagh. My Maynooth doctoral dissertation had been on 'The Anglican Doctrine of the Church in the Tudor Period' and left me with such a serious fascination with ecumenism that my first full-length book was entitled *Roman Catholics and Unity* (1962), and published at the invitation of the editor of a series on ecumenism, Bishop Oliver Tomkins of Bristol, and Chair, as I remember, of the World Council of Churches' Faith and Order Commission.

The second theme which took hold at the time was the relation between Church and State and the issue of religious freedom. This was sparked by a family interest in politics and given shape in my post graduate days at Maynooth through involvement with a group of young lay, intellectual and politically minded graduates concerned with the economic, social and political difficulties of the Ireland of the 1950s. The group which had been named 'Tuairim' (Irish for opinion or view) opened me up to new ways of examining such issues including the role of the Church in our divided Ireland. It also left me with some very close and permanent friendships. A little earlier I had encountered the work of American Jesuit John Courtney Murray whose writings, which I found so liberating, led to his being silenced by Rome in the 1950s, though he later provided the basis for the *Declaration on Religious Liberty* at Vatican II in 1965.

The third lasting theme was not, as I had anticipated, the relation between science and religion but that between the arts and religion. I had been an enthusiastic student of Theoretical Physics for my primary degree and had serious intentions of following it up. My Archbishop decided otherwise and by then I was deeply involved in theology. However, an earlier (in primary and secondary school) and continuing interest in the arts, particularly poetry and theatre, became another intellectual interlocutor with theology and politics.

Travels in Theology

1. A European Education

After a year concentrating mainly on Aquinas at the Angelicum University in Rome but free to take in Stanislas Lyonnet at the Biblicum and Frederick Copleston at the Gregorian, I had an unexpected and irrevocable career change. I was appointed as Professor of Moral Theology at Maynooth and requested to do a doctorate in Canon Law so that I could fill the portfolio of Professor of Canon Law as well. Diocesan priests at least were obedient fellows in those days and so back to Rome for Canon Law at the Gregorian and a two-year licence to be achieved in one. No great satisfaction in that, but now that I knew my academic destiny I could look around a little for help and instruction to the Alphonsianum with Bernhard Häring and brilliant Irish Redemptorist, Seán O Riordan, also a Maynooth doctorate, and to that kindliest of theologians at the Gregorianum, Joseph Fuchs SJ, where one of my companions was friend and later colleague, Vincent Mac Namara. Fuchs' seminar on the Law of Christ was one of the best I attended.

A year of Canon Law at the Gregorianum, despite the helpfulness of the Dean of Canon Law, Dutchman Piet Huizing, gave me a taste for wider horizons and after obtaining my licence I was accepted at the faculty in Munich for my doctorate. I had realised that my doctoral proposal on Church–State relations was not very acceptable to the youngish Jesuit teaching Public Ecclesiastical Law in Rome, the area which dealt with Church – State relations. So I was pleased to find that Professor Klaus Moersdorf at Munich was open to the proposal and so he remained, although he deeply disagreed with my views and those of John Courtney Murray.

Rome was more an ecclesial, historical and cultural influence than a theological one. That was due in part to the fact that I was not formally studying theology but philosophy, Aquinas style, in my first year, and canon law in the second.

The death of Pius XII and the election of John XXIII deepened one's awareness of the history and universality of the Church. And in spite of various restrictions on clerical leisure activity, the city and museums were there for the seeing and the concerts for the listening. For contact between religion and the arts one had only to look around the monuments were everywhere. Yet such theology as I heard from professors or students was not in any serious dialogue with the arts. The monuments themselves provided a continuing history of pagan and Christian Rome and its culture.

Munich, for all its cultural resources, could not compete at that level with Rome. For a student serious about the theological sciences in themselves and in dialogue with other university and secular disciplines, it was fresh and stimulating. Effective entry into the world of German theological scholarship in 1959 had deep and enduring consequences, although inevitably one began to appreciate the weaknesses as well as the strengths as the years went by and other intellectual and cultural influences, including the Irish, began to assume new importance.

In Schmaus (Dogmatics), Schmidt (New Testament), Egenter (Moral) and of course my director in Canon Law, Moersdorf, Munich had true scholars whose lectures and seminars I sometimes managed to attend when my canon law obligations permitted. Romano Guardini was in his last semester when I arrived and although in frail health still attracted large audiences including myself when I could get a seat. The completion of my dissertation on 'Church–State Relations with Particular Reference to the Irish Constitution' was the main element in my theological/canonical development at that time. However, exposure to the German university and theological system as well as to the city of Munich and its culture had a marked influence. Theological and social exchanges with professors and other graduate students were part of a wider education and paved the way for deeper involvement in German theological life later. Moral theologian Richard Egenter was particularly helpful in introducing me to the 'Association of German-speaking Moral Theologians' in the 1960s where I met many theologians from Eastern Europe, still of course under Soviet control. For a mixture of reasons my reading in German theology ranged far beyond the writings of contemporary moral theologians such as Bernhard Häring, Joseph Fuchs, Alfons Auer, Franz Boeckle and, a little later, Bruno Schuller and Klaus Demmer, and into the earlier works of renewal by Fritz Tillmann, scripture scholar turned moral theologian.

However, dogmatic theologians and scripture scholars from across Europe such as Karl Rahner and his German successors, for example J.B. Metz, Hans Küng, Joseph Ratzinger, Dutch Dominican Edward Schillebeeckx, French Dominicans Congar and Chenu and their Jesuit compatriots, de Lubac and Danielou, Scripture scholars like Lyonnet, Schnackenburg and Spicq, all these and others I regarded as essential reading for the reintegration of moral theology into theology as a whole. This was the first task confronting me as I began to teach theology in 1960. It remains a continuing and critical task.

Because of the strong Irish influence at every level in the Catholic Church in Britain one could, as an Irish theologian, easily miss its distinctiveness in theological terms as well as its European dimension. These were both cultural and ecclesial. Engagement with the Catholic Marriage Advisory Council and its leading members, Director, Father Maurice O'Leary, and medical–theological experts such as Drs John Marshall and Jack Dominian, helped provide the beginnings of a new vision of sex and marriage which moral theology badly needed. This was further developed at annual conferences convened by Cardinal Suenens in Brussels from the early 1960s. A quite different process was initiated in the Ecumenical Moral Theology group which Professor Gordon Dunstan of King's College, London, and I established in the early 1960s and which included Scots and Welsh, Presbyterian and Methodist as well as Anglican and Catholic. A volume of papers from various meetings of the group was published in the late 1960s.

Friendship and scholarship combined in both Oxford and Cambridge with Catholics such as Herbert Mc Cabe and Nicholas Lash and Anglicans such as John Macquarrie and Donald Mac Kinnon and in the broader theological world with colleagues like Kevin Kelly. Through these interchanges broader and deeper theological concerns were at work than might be considered within the remit of even a renewed moral theology. God, suffering and salvation, ecclesiology and ecumenism, sacrament and society, secularity and religion, prayer and praxis were some of the topics which, although not regular in moral theological discourse, could and did, we hoped, enrich it.

2. Transatlantic Perspectives

In the history of the United States of America 1963 was a crucial year. In the high summer of that year there was the great Washington Civil Rights' March with Martin Luther King's 'I have a dream'. In the melancholy late Autumn the dream seemed more nightmare with the assassination of President John F. Kennedy. From June through August I paid my first theological visit to the US. Teaching Summer School at the Catholic University of America in Washington DC in the heat and humidity was far from pleasant, but students and staff colleagues were delightfully refreshing. Although the Catholic Church in America was, in the recent judgment of one of its own significant historians, John Tracey Ellis, undistinguished intellectually if not downright anti-intellectual, there were exciting theological stirrings on the campuses and among the colleagues I visited on that trip from Washington to St Louis to St John's, Minnesota to Boston and New York. The energy and insight available wherever I went over the next decades have never ceased to amaze and, I trust, enrich me. The experience of teaching mature women students and a little later of having women colleagues of the highest calibre gradually connected very closely in my own development with the major lessons of that tumultuous year. Racism and its destructiveness, the possibility of overcoming gross and centuries-old oppression and injustice by peaceful means and under Christian inspiration, the ecumenical alliances and the imaginative strategies so courageously undertaken by Martin Luther King and the Civil Rights Movement, became life-long intellectual and practical obsessions, particularly in relation to Northern Ireland and Southern Africa.

Over a period of forty years theological trips to North and Central America and the Caribbean yielded valuable fruit, both in what one approved of and in what one disapproved of. To a moral theologian increasingly preoccupied with justice and peace in the world, US political and economic power seemed more and more a negative influence. There were, of course, many notable personal and policy exceptions to this destructiveness over the decades. Many theologians and other academics, intellectuals and, especially, artists opposed the most negative of these policies. Many did not. Church leadership became entangled too often with single and, predominantly, sex-related issues such as contraception, divorce, homosexuality, abortion, condom use even in the face of the AIDS pandemic etc. to give clear leadership on poverty, peace and other social issues even in their own country. Northern neighbour Canada was often a more comfortable place for the travelling moral theologian, while Central America and the Caribbean countries stuck world poverty and exploitation right under one's nose. A continuing regret is that through a series of mishaps the theological travels never penetrated further south into the Latin American home countries of Liberation Theology. Meeting these theologians elsewhere and reading their work was only the next best thing, but still very helpful.

Africa, Asia and Australia

Without Africa where would any of us be? Indeed would any of us *be*? If somewhere on that landmass humanity took its first faltering but upright steps, and home is where we start from in Eliot's phrase, we are coming home when we land on African soil. That has at least been my increasing conviction since I first went there with Bishop Christopher Butler in the summer (ours) of 1970 to offer the Catholic Churches in South Africa and Lesotho a series of Winter (theirs) Schools in Theology. Thirty-five years and more than twenty visits later, some of them quite extended, it would be exaggerating to consider Africa as my most influential theological teacher, but influential it certainly has been. The sense of homecoming may have taken time to settle down, perhaps only really occurring during the summer stints studying the civil-war/war-of-independence in Rhodesia/Zimbabwe between 1973 and 1978, and coming to full fruition during the working trips in the fight against HIV and AIDS sponsored by Caritas Internationalis and CAFOD, London from 1990 onwards. In the very different contexts of theology workshops and of retreats, of war, famine and plague with their horrors matched only by the resilience of so many people, I began to find a God and feel a hope that had seemed lost in the shallows of my other home life. I began to find new reasons and perhaps new methods for theology.

The message of the Gospels is a message of salvation and so a message of healing. The first impact of Africa on the naïve and vain European was that he was bringing the healing for all the ills of paganism and other religious distortions, of poverty, corruption and war, of AIDS and a host of other diseases and privations. And some of that was true, but could only be Gospel truth and effective healing if the European began to recognise his own need for healing and his past and present roles in spreading and sustaining the many ills now afflicting African peoples. From colonialism and its political and economic exploitation through racism and apartheid to the surrogate wars promoted by the great powers of two centuries, the European and Western record makes painful reading for the visitor, if not to be compared with the painful suffering of the indigenous peoples. Many Christian missionaries did their best to mitigate these sufferings but they did so, by and large and for a long time, under the shelter of the exploiting and colonial powers. It would be humanly demeaning of Africans to ignore their responsibility for some of the present distress. But politically, militarily and economically on their own continent, they have been an underclass for several centuries, deprived of power and of the responsibility that goes with it.

The European tradition of theology, Anselm's 'faith seeking understanding' was the classic description of a theologian's work. For a long time it seemed to me better to keep the Pauline triad together and speak of 'faith-hope-love seeking understanding' where that understanding could not be achieved by intellectual effort only but also by the practice of love of God and neighbour, and through that love the birthing and nourishing of hope. As involvement in Africa grew, mindful loving service assumed a priority which helped to keep despair at bay for the visiting servant and sometimes at least helped develop hope for the local people. Faith still sought understanding but the faith and the understanding were dependent on the love and hope which the Christian community of locals and strangers was developing.

I hesitate to describe this as liberation theology, as if indeed there were just one kind of liberation theology. Yet in origin and in method it belongs to that family. This mainly African-shaped practice of theology has also been partly responsible for my hesitation in describing myself as a moral theologian, in any conventional sense at any rate. Perhaps all theologians are now called to escape the pigeonholes of the traditional disciplines of scripture, systematic, moral etc. and accept the call to be theologians in a broader sense with particular interests and experiences in which they acquire sharper skills with deeper knowledge and understanding.

My theological trips to Asia were motivated in much the same way as those to Africa: to be of practical educational help, particularly in facing the HIV and AIDS pandemic, and often followed similar patterns, allowing for the cultural and religious differences. Yet these very cultural and religious differences affected the theological visitor in some interestingly different ways. The remnants of colonialism still showed. The poverty, corruption and oppression, from within and without, dominated the areas of concern to us. And war or the legacy of war was often very evident. But just then the visitor was forced to consider also the legacy of Gandhi, the still active influence of the Dalai Lama and the Asian contributions to a civilisation of peace as well as of war. Although it was mainly through the conflicts in Northern Ireland and Zimbabwe that I began to appreciate the horrors of armed struggle, it was in the few Asian countries in which I worked that I finally became convinced of the possibility and the necessity of alternatives to war in the twenty-first century. The theological campaign which Stanley Hauerwas, Linda Hogan and myself have been recently promoting owes something at least to Asian exposure.

The second significant shift in theological thinking after Asia did not of course originate there. But like the reaction to war it emerged much more clearly there. And to continue the reshaping of theology from 'faith seeking understanding' to 'love, hope, faith seeking understanding', the new shape would have to make much more explicit reference to prayer and to contemplative prayer without losing its practical and intellectual dimensions.

The short-lived and mainly casual encounters with the contemplative element in Buddhism and other Asian religions which these visits to Thailand, Burma, Hong Kong, the Philippines and Japan permitted could only provide the stimulus for attempting the conversion of theology to a seriously contemplative activity. However, the challenge can no longer be evaded. An earlier discovery of the significance of the liturgy for Christian living and moral theology could not and had not neglected the importance of personal prayer and contemplation. However, the Asian experience renewed the sense of contemplation as essential to the theologian.

Beyond Asia's geographical, cultural and religious boundaries lay those paradoxical outposts of the West, Australia and New Zealand. One of the joke competitions of my post-graduate days in Dunboyne House at Maynooth offered a prize for the shortest possible theological work. One of the winners was 'A Theological Analysis of Limbo', but the overall winner came from an Australian and was entitled 'The Australian Book of Mysticism'. To young Irish theological snobs it sounded a winner. On my first theological trip to Australia I was presented with a beautiful book entitled, *The Australian Book of Religious Verse* edited by Les Murray. This was the real thing and a real winner. I was already familiar with some of the Australian poets, novelists and artists through Australian friends picked up along the way. But the impact of this book was amazing and a perfect cure for any residual Irish religious arrogance. It was hard to cope with the sometimes offensive pragmatism of Australian politics, the popular addiction to sport of all kinds and the conservatism of much of the hierarchical Church. Yet the vitality and beauty of its artistic life with perhaps the Sydney Opera House as its key symbol plus the intelligence and energy of so much of its pastoral and theological life were very appealing. And one was not allowed by the people I mixed with to forget the unresolved problems of the Aboriginal peoples, their religious and artistic achievements.

This was not something I was made aware of in the same way in the US, although it had affected the theological and ecclesial consciousness in Canada and still more in New Zealand.

The point of this theological travelogue, if it has one, is to emphasise that much as I love books and libraries, a great deal of what shaped my theological life I received from the people, events and places I encountered in my travels as a believer in search of the God of creation and incarnation, of passion, death and resurrection, of the God of the 'drunken variousness' of people, places, ideas as well as things, as Irish poet, Louis McNeice nearly, but more neatly, put it.

The End of All Our Exploring

Theology is never a single journey with just one destination in mind. There are incessant comings and goings, intellectual and spiritual as well as in this case the geographical, political and cultural changes which all these travels entail. Yet if home was where we started from, in the deeper sense as applied to all humanity, that for me was Africa. Yet to quote again, 'the end of all our exploring/Will be to arrive where we started/And know the place for the first time'. And that for me was Ireland, Maynooth and Mayo. And of course most of my theological life from First Divinity in Maynooth was, despite all the travel, spent in Ireland. As I now look for distinctive Irish influences I mention only a few of the more important. The sense of the margins and of people at the margins of society and Church began for me in Mayo and has only been reinforced by theological travels and reflections. The Irish imagination and its companion beauty, particularly as expressed in literature, have made me receptive to other peoples and cultures and above all to ways of doing theology which are continually pushing one to transcend one's present self and one's present work. And for me and my theology the oft-quoted phrase of British Chief Secretary for Ireland (c.1900), Augustine Birrell, 'It is the Mass that matters' still applies. A eucharistic (moral) theology combines liturgy, word and life in material–symbolic, personal–communitarian, transcendent and transforming ways.

Fortunately, all those influences, Irish and global, are still active. Their impact has affected teaching and writing over the past fifty years. And as one lives in hope, the spring-board of all fresh theology, there may be a little more to come. Yet as Maurya, the tragic mother in Synge's beautiful and great play, *Riders to the Sea*, puts it at the conclusion of her grieving for the death by drowning of her sixth and last son: 'No man at all can be living for ever, And we must be satisfied'.

12.

Journeying with Moral Theology

Vincent MacNamara

They would not believe you, young theologians today, if you told them that in the 1950s and 1960s it was widely accepted that one who was preparing to teach moral theology would need to study canon law. That was how I started, though not through any choice of my own. That was in Maynooth. I was lucky in ways, because I found myself in an unusually gifted group of postgraduates, most of them doing theology and some of them inveterately addicted to late-night theological discussion. It was a time when the first faint whisperings of renewal in moral theology were coming to our shores.

It was in that context that I came in contact with Häring's *The Law of Christ* – in French. It had not yet been translated into English and I did not yet read German. It not only opened up for us new thinking but put us in touch with an earlier neglected tradition – Tillmann, Mausbach etc. – which had existed in Germany since the 1940s, alongside the dominant and arid neo-Scholasticism. Perhaps, more than anything else, Häring and like-minded authors liberated moral theology from canon law, freeing it to be itself. It did not matter to us then that the renewal was kerygmatic in tone and content, and lacking in rigour, or that its use of scripture was naïve. It opened the windows.

It was a piece of good fortune for me – and perhaps for them, I don't know – that two of my professors were made bishops, so that the canon law faculty could not function without its quota of five doctors. So I was on my way to Rome to finish my doctorate in canon law. That did not distract me from attending a theology course that was to be influential for me. On the back of Enda McDonagh's stuttering scooter, I went to hear the young Josef Fuchs at the Gregorian. He was giving a course on the interiority of the new law in Aquinas. For those of us reared on the precepts of the manual it was fascinating and revolutionary. I think we felt that we were at the dawn of something.

I soon found myself back in Ireland teaching moral theology in a large theologate – caught half-way between the old manuals and the heady stuff from Häring, Fuchs and Aquinas. The phrase I remember best from that time was 'the glorious freedom of the children of God', something beloved of the new theology. I used to tell my moralist colleagues that it was all very well for them to announce that with abandon. But, as well as teaching theology, I had to run a seminary with its usual quota of rules and regulations. There were plenty of opportunities to test whether this glorious freedom worked in practice.

The renewal of moral theology was confirmed by Vatican II with its insistence that scripture was to be its soul. The call seemed to be to get back to the idyllic picture of the early church and to escape the soul-sapping casuistry of the manual. There was fundamental reshaping. Out went the manual to be replaced by a loose amalgam of scriptural themes. The central thrust was to be the centrality of love – a retrieval of Aquinas's position that charity is the form of all the virtues. Of course, philosophical personalism was in the air, anyway – Häring had written on a personalist approach to natural law. Gilleman's illuminating work from a few decades earlier, *The Primacy of Charity in Moral Theology*, came into its own.

Other themes broadened the agenda for moral theology. I found myself peddling to my students a diet, no doubt indigestible, of Schillebeckx, Congar, Rahner, Metz, de Chardin and Gutierrez. They had opened up new and dynamic visions of the very agenda of moral theology. So you could not escape theologies of work, of progress, of the laity, of earthly realities, of the kingdom, of development, of hope, of justice, of liberation. It had the effect of healing the old breach between systematic and moral theology.

But then came a stunning blow. I remember exactly where I was when the news of *Humanae Vitae* broke and the chilling feeling that a cloud of confusion and resentment was about to descend on us. Life was to become more difficult not only for Catholics generally but for moral theologians. What followed was a shabby period of desperate appeal to apparent modifications from this or that episcopal conference, or stratagems to ease the severity of the teaching. The worst prejudices about casuistry were revived. And it goes on. Glaring issues about AIDS have further eroded trust.

At the end of the 1960s I found myself back in Rome formally studying moral theology. Fuchs was a key figure. He had two great concerns: the method of Christian moral theology, particularly the implications of the new-found interest in the Bible as a starting point; and the question of moral absolutes. A seminar on absolutes became crucial not only for his postgraduate students but for himself. I remember the rigorously organised weekly sessions and testing week ends of discussion in a villa in the Alban hills.

Catholic moral theology had been strong on absolutes – think of almost anything in the area of sexual ethics. And the related issues were far-reaching – sacred principles like that of double effect and of intrinsic evil were proving increasingly unsatisfactory and needed reworking. In the literature, the approaches to such questions among Catholics were few and tentative. That seminar issued for Fuchs himself, as he often told, in a famous and influential article in *Gregorianum* entitled 'The Absoluteness of Moral Terms'.[1] It had a liberating effect. It gave us confidence to tangle with the thorny problem of norms and exceptions. That was to engage me quite a bit. The debate remains acute – witness *Veritatis Splendor*.

Fuchs was also a key figure in another development which questioned the naiveté of the rush to Scripture and which produced what came to be known as the theory of an autonomous ethic within Christianity, the other side of the debate being known as the faith-ethic. In its crude form (many of its exponents modified their positions later) it said that, in terms of material norms, there is nothing in Christian morality that is not available to non-Christians – and nothing in the Bible. It became for many an issue encapsulated in the question whether there is such a thing as a specific Christian morality. The debate between the two sides was extraordinarily bitter, the autonomy school being accused of undermining Christianity and the teaching authority of the church.

That debate remained an interest for me. So that when I returned to Ireland and more teaching – this time mainly at Maynooth – I wondered more and more about method. It struck me that our problem was part of a wider problem to which we had given little attention. Namely, the very issue of a religious morality: 'What are the implications of that conjunction of words?' or 'What are the relations between religion and morality?' I could find little discussion of that in Catholic circles.

Not long afterwards I had the chance to go to Oxford. I undertook an analysis there of the recent history of Catholic moral theology – what I saw as a biblical renewal, a reaction to that and a floundering on the issue of method. But what was more important for me in Oxford was its school of philosophy. So that while I was meant to be working on my thesis – and I was – I sat in on every philosophy course I could manage – Strawson, Mackie, Hare, Hart, Kenny, Warnock and many others (and extramurally, and by way of contrast, on Herbert McCabe's engrossing night course in Blackfriars on the moral teaching of Aquinas).

I don't know how much I learned from all this mainly analytical philosophy, but I think it helped my thinking about issues that had been bothering me – the language of morals, the structure of the moral act, key notions of intention, reason, motive, logic, justification and so on. I was conscious of the fact that philosophers generally, and even those sympathetic to the enterprise of religious ethics, were critical of what they saw as the methodological shambles of moral theology.[2] It was true that there had been little analysis of terms and meanings. I did find it in Bruno Schüller, who had an interest in Anglo-American philosophy and – perhaps not surprisingly for those who knew of their traditional engagement with philosophical logic – in some Polish Catholic moralists.

The issue was one of credibility – the soggy language and approach of the renewal had not helped. Theologians carried along by enthusiasm for the new scriptural approach needed to listen to what was happening in the thriving science of hermeneutics. It is to their credit that many of them came to do so: it is instructive, for example, to compare the early and late Häring.

I was in sympathy with the autonomy point of view, especially with its desire to find common cause with the best of secular morality and with its more critical stance towards the use of scripture. But I was not entirely satisfied. The bearing of religious considerations on the moral subject's perception of reality, and therefore of moral values, seemed to me to be understated. I was particularly struck by the approaches of James Gustafson with his espousal of a faith-discernment that is contextual, situated in a tradition at a given point in its history, of Iris Murdoch with her interest in the significance of vision and inner life for morality, and of Alasdair MacIntyre with his stance that there is no sphere of morality independent of the agent's metaphysical or theological (or anti-theological) view of the world. My leanings were confirmed for me by a growing literature in comparative cultural and ethical studies, especially comparative religious ethics, for which it was axiomatic that one cannot understand a moral system unless one understands the web of beliefs, stories and practices in which it is inserted. Our basic myths shape our meanings: cosmogony affects ethical order.[3] One who subscribes to a religion is likely to experience the influence of its overarching world-view on moral perception.

The issue of whether there is a specific Christian ethic may have been flogged almost to death – by me, among others. The question may have been badly stated. But the central concern remains: how does adherence to a religious myth and a religious community shape one's morality – if it does? The way forward, I think, is more dialogue about the logic of religious ethics in general (one therefore hopes that theology in the university will not isolate itself from religious studies). And attention to a matter which is inseparable from it, i.e. how does a religious community's, indeed any community's, ethical vision fare in the marketplace in a pluralist society – what William Frankena described as 'one of the central issues of our cultural crisis'?[4] That is something that looms ever larger for us in a multicultural Ireland.

That was one dimension of my theological story. There was another. The day job for me was teaching moral theology in various theological institutes. Like many theologians in the sixties and seventies, I also found myself involved in courses to interested lay people through the country and abroad. And I had my own, if limited, pastoral experience here in Ireland and elsewhere. What struck me most was the need for liberation. Not liberation from morality: morality is inescapable, always makes its claim and is never easy. But liberation from a constricting – and cruel – notion of what morality is about.

The current morality was held down with the steel hawsers of precept/merit/reward/punishment, what Rahner had called the law-court model. It stunted people's lives. What of the glorious liberty of the children of God, what of the interiority of the new law in Paul and Aquinas? It was a moral system which made people fearful and anxious and childish – anyone who ever sat in a confession box in the 1950s or 1960s knows that. And from which my church has reaped a bitter harvest of resentment and anger. To offer an approach to morality that saw it rather as the invitation or task of listening to our own humanity, of being human together, of caring for a society of humanness, seemed to me to be a project for the emerging generation of moralists. This was something, indeed, not just for a Christian notion of morality but for a Christian notion of God. So there was a challenge to write about morality in a fashion that made contact with people's experience.

I was also brought to wonder more about the moral agent and less about moral acts. The old manual dealt sketchily with problems affecting the individual – ignorance, force, fear and so on. But, by and large, moral teaching was locked in formulae. It had a stereotype of the person that seemed to take for granted that everybody could appreciate moral issues and respond to them, if only they had goodwill. But understanding of the person had been revolutionised since the days when Palmieri and Ballerini swapped footnotes: Freud, Jung and Lacan were insisting that people are in no way like the flat figure of the moral text-book.

My interest here was deepened when I had the good fortune to come under the influence of, and later to work with, the Irish Dominican, Miceál O'Regan, founder of Eckhart House, a wise, witty and gifted psychologist and psychotherapist, with an extraordinary knowledge of the variety of spiritual traditions. His project was to explore the middle ground between the insights of modern psychology and the insights of the great spiritual traditions. I liked that. His interest in the mystery and the becoming of the person seemed to me to interlock with the moralist's concern for human flourishing – to use a word that for many had come to express the heart of morality.

So I found myself wondering further about the dynamism of the human person, about the puzzle of human desire, about the different levels of the desiring subject, about the fragmentation that is the lot of all of us, about the impossibility of integration, about difference. About the forest of the mind. About where wisdom lay. I had once seen Iris Murdoch being interviewed on television: to the suggestion that there were some very strange people in her books she calmly replied that what goes on in our own minds and our own hearts is more strange than anything in her books. Point taken. The heart is a wonder. We are enmeshed in the patterns we have unconsciously grown into since our first awakening. You could say that we do not know who we are, or why we do what we do. We are at permanent risk of self-delusion. A morality that does not in some fashion to take that into account is in denial. So I continue to wonder and explore.

Psychology and psychoanalysis were to be taken more seriously but so were the other sciences, anthropology, for example. A man once said to me at a seminar in Africa, 'No matter what we start discussing here, we always end up with polygamy'. He could have added other questions which bothered his colleagues about the nature, form and celebration of marriage and so on. That kind of engagement with the meeting of faith and cultures is an obvious challenge and it is a matter of regret to me that the Irish missionary movement has not managed to free up theological thought in such contexts.

But there is so much that challenges today. Nobody doing theology could be insulated from postmodernism, from concern with the social construction of reality, from women's studies, from the biomedical revolution, from environmental and justice issues, from debate about human nature. We cannot just batten down the hatches: it is not a matter of applying well-worn formulae to emerging situations. The intersection of faith and culture is a two-way process. What Christian faith and its related moral response mean at a particular time and place has to be discovered. We have to believe that God is not locked in the past but is with us in history. We do not know what is ahead. Like all Christians, theologians travel in hope.

How to offer, especially to the younger generation, a convincing perspective on values in the midst of our cultural upheaval – and I think it is values rather than rules that should concern us – becomes for me ever more critically important. We need to do some re-imagining. We find ourselves in the dangerous waters between an absolutism that is culturally and historically naïve and a relativism that makes any kind of normative claim suspect. I continue to hope, however, that, in dialogue with the sciences, we can suggest a way forward that is realistic, sympathetic, street-wise and that nonetheless knows the depth and breadth of the human spirit. Human life has certain ineradicable and defining characteristics that are commensurable from one social or historical context to another – but analogously. The human community can dialogue across ages and cultures in its ongoing search. Christianity has its wisdom to offer to that dialogue.

Notes

1. *Gregorianum* 52/3, 1971.
2. See G.J. Hughes, *Authority in Morals* (London: Heythrop, 1978), William Frankena, 'Is Morality Logically Dependent on Religion?' in G. Outka and J.P. Reeder Jr. (eds), *Religion and Morality* (New York: Anchor, 1973) 295ff.
3. See, for example, Robin W. Lovin and Frank E. Reynolds (eds.) *Cosmogony and Ethical Order: New Studies in Comparative Ethics* (Chicago: University of Chicago Press, 1985).
4. Ibid., p. 295.

13.

Alive and Signalling: Theology as Calling

Geraldine Smyth

It may be a truism that theology finds its first home in religious experience. Christian theology is certainly inconceivable detached from revelation, faith, tradition and history – each and together involving complex processes. In reflecting on keynote life influences on my theology, I naturally look first to my family and the early formative experiences of home, parish church and school as the *fons et origens* of faith; then, to the Dominican Order as second family, home-base of my adult religious life and the point of departure for involvement in a number of fields which have significantly intersected with my theological interests. For, of course, theology must never disengage from its ground in religious faith.

Fellow Northerner, Seamus Heaney, recollects sitting on the arm of the kitchen sofa, listening to sound-waves from the wireless – foreign-sounding names, accents and the fictional discourse of strange places and times – clashing in his childhood imagination with the dialect and diction of family and neighbourhood. Thus his native 'den-like existence' which seemed 'more or less emotionally and intellectually proofed against the outside world', was interrupted by voices which bore him 'on a journey into the wideness of the world ... and the wideness of language'. For even then, '[he] was already being schooled ... for the reality of violence ... world history and world-sorrow behind it' that before long would become a familiar feature of his Ulster context.[1] Thus, the vitality of the poet's public voice has never ceased to depend on that fertile exchange between the 'alive and signalling' language of childhood and the sophistications of the literary world. This rings true for me as a Christian theologian. Our origins travel with us, not as cultural baggage *tout simple*, but as a vibrant, inhabited 'underworld', in constant recursive interaction with the other, contesting, and second-level discourses. They provide a rudimentary compass through the crisscrossing of bonds, boundaries, ruptures and adventures that shape our values and influence our ways of life.[2]

Not long ago a visit to my old parish church knocked me off my theological perch. I 'caught myself on' bringing my hand in unbroken gesture from St Anthony's foot to forehead as the preliminary to blessing myself. The reflex of manifest devotion called forth a reflex blush, followed by a recollection of the significance of St John's, Belfast – place of my baptism, first communion and confirmation; the example of saintly or cross-faced elders encouraging or reprimanding; memories stirred of my seven-year-old daily visits to the confessional. Far from being scrupulous, I had gleaned that more important than the focus on sin, confession 'invites us into a personal encounter with Christ'. I recalled the ensuing conflict of interpretations with the parish priest, who – unimpressed by such theological precocity – laid down that once-a-week was sufficient. Such is the deep-grained influence that this pre-critical, textured world, 'thick' with mediations of religious culture,[3] had worked on my religious imagination and outlook, nurturing 'a sense and taste for the infinite'. Much of it would later be subjected to scrutiny, rebelled against or rejected. Some aspects would be retrieved and re-interpreted within a different framework and context, after the manner of Paul Ricoeur's affirming the significance of a second naiveté as conviction passes through critique, chastened and reappropriated.[4]

I moved freely between the kindred points of home and the outer boundaries of neighbourhood, culture and religion.

Sunday Mass was the accepted norm, but beyond that, my parents showed appreciation for difference of temperament and interest, encouraging us to find and follow our unique paths – socially, in sports or in diverse careers. There was an unspoken sense that as Catholics we had more to overcome to find our rightful place. At nine I joined the parish choir and remember the aesthetic appeal of the eucharistic mystery whether through High Mass or Lenten devotions. It is the tremulous associations of heads bent in prayer, the purple-shrouded crucifix, Mozart's *Ave Verum,* the 'smell' of the *Tantum Ergo* that remain, more than the fiery sermons. My interest in liturgical life was rooted here.

Ecumenical questions started early. With an Anglican grand-father, exchange with Protestant relations was commonplace. A Greek Orthodox uncle and my father's Jewish business colleagues lent further spice to family visits. My ecumenical questioning was aroused. At a Dominican high school, the search for truth was linked to the ideal of *veritas* and the belief that grace fulfils nature. Our sixth year Religious Education teacher, fresh from *Lumen Vitae* in Belgium, introduced theology as 'faith in search of understanding' together with the biblical approach of salvation history. We explored Aquinas's Five Ways and debated the need for the church to adapt to changing culture. We appealed to Paul's defiance of Peter on this topic with the ringing phrase – 'I resisted him to his face' (Gal 2:11). It was the mid-1960s: existentialism, the novels of Camus and Murdoch, Mauriac's *Life of St Teresa of Avila* were daily bread. Paisley's sectarian polemic was stirring on the streets, although the campaign for civil rights and 'The Troubles' remained in the wings. Martin Luther King's civil rights movement, the Sharpeville protest and massacre appalled and found local resonance. Foundations were shifting. We felt ourselves a new generation with responsibilities for nuclear disarmament, social justice and human rights. The *aggiornamento* of Vatican II was heralding new possibilities of bringing the church to the heart of the modern world. For me, however, the turn to society was put on hold. The novitiate beckoned. My theological life was beginning in earnest.

I owe to my years of formation in 'Religious Life' more than can be said here: the reality of a personal relationship with Christ, deepening understanding of the world as revelation of the divine and of human desire as the doorway to holiness. Life in common taught me that the church's mission is strong when community is a lived reality. The encouragement to dwell in 'the cell of self-knowledge' (Catherine of Siena's term) – through the discipline of study, silence, *lectio divina* – held theological implications that became clearer later, especially in my work in Eckhart House, which embodied an approach to the person that brought together the insights of transpersonal psychology and incarnational theology. Religious formation nurtured the sense of the sacred, through contemplative presence and the practice of meditation. *Novare me, novare te.* God was very near. This pattern of living into the sacred, of prayers of blessing over daily actions, I would later discover as a spiritual bond with Jewish Halakhic spirituality or Eastern practice, thus offering a bridge of ecumenical understanding. The difficulties and delight inherent in community living have helped keep my ecumenism grounded. The struggle to live reconciliation amid the simple generosities, pettinesses, self-deceptions which thrive in any quasi-closed system proved a salutary reminder to me as an ecumenical theologian that we can expect the ecumenical journey likewise to be fraught with rivalry or difficulties of honesty (that have little to do with theological truth); yet often surprising us with the gesture of compassion or tact – grace fulfilling nature.[5]

Theological study in Maynooth brought the testing that is characteristic of the journey of faith. These were the years of post-Vatican II change, marked by theological challenge and excitement. Teachers like Enda McDonagh, Kevin MacNamara, Seán Freyne and Flan Markham (men all the way!) shared a theological vision that inspired and opened themes and dynamics of the relationship of revelation, faith, reason, experience and tradition. Students debated with passion as to how the seminary ethos would prevail in an expanded NUI college or re-imagine itself as an ecclesial centre of formation within the projected secular academy. As one of the small cohort of lay students and sisters, I found the heaviness of the clerical institutional culture at variance with the theological vision expressed in the programme. One felt an outsider – believing (not without struggle) but not belonging.

Paradoxically, it was in the secular University of Ulster, reading English, that I would find bridges between faith and culture in a time of rapid change. Secularist friends seemed pained on my behalf that I was 'burying myself in a religious order'. As the only 'nun' on campus, dislodged from the rhythms of vocational life with its confessional language, I came to value their interrogation of my purpose and suppositions, thus inviting me to give an account of my hope. I found an existential entry into debates on 'religionless Christianity,' the 'death of God' or 'the secular city'.[6] There were unlikely conjunctions of spirit – as with two Protestant students (a Monarchist and a Buddhist!): our comparisons between Buddhist and Christian accounts of desire or detachment, the need for attentiveness and the correspondences between *metta* and *agape* were instinct with the thrill of the strange, bringing an urge to cross religious boundaries or explore unsettling philosophical questions and political diversities. Reading Paul Tillich prompted an intuition that when the time came for further theological studies, this boundary of faith and culture would attract my attention both analytically and practically.[7]

My years teaching English and RE were in the denominationally mixed Dominican College, Portstewart. The varieties of teaching experience – whether exploring the clash of doubt and faith in Dostoevsky's *Grand Inquisitor* scene with sixth formers, or despairing at the look of studied *ennui* on their faces as I tried to drum up interest on the significance of the sacrament of marriage – put me to the pin of my wimple. I became more insistently aware of the necessary engagement between faith and culture, opposing those who mooted the idea that we Dominicans should abandon teaching secular subjects, if not the running of educational institutions altogether, and concentrate exclusively on evangelisation. To me, such withdrawal was possessed of neither educational sense nor theological integrity. I could not conceive but that encounter with the world of classical texts – poem, play or novel – had an irreducible role in enabling students to refine their own capacity for empathetic imagination, to grow in moral discernment between truthfulness and false-seeming, or to be creative and humble in the face of conflict or suffering. I used often return to Paul's admonition (Phil 4:4–9) that we should turn our minds to *whatever* is true, *whatever* beautiful or good or just.

Then, and later, living in Belfast, sectarian violence was relentless. None of us was untouched at a personal level (two of my cousins were shot, one fatally). As communities we sheltered evacuated families, comforted pupils whose parents had been murdered, attended funeral on funeral, dismayed at the apparent failure of the churches to act significantly beyond offering pastoral care to their own. One Saturday, I found a long remote-control command wire in the school grounds, ready for detonating when the routine foot-patrol passed. Senseless, yes. But such actions were driven too by their own *a priori* logic that put itself beyond question.

At this time, meeting with Miceál O'Regan and being involved in the founding of Eckhart House, was another grace, teaching me much about living with limits and welcoming difference – including within the self. Here was another experience of the middle ground, rooted in a community of meditative practice and professional service – a field of discourse where insights of modern psychology, theological anthropology and Christian practice found forms of mutual address in the human search for meaning, healing and responsibility. From these distinct perspectives in dialogue, I began to understand the futility of striving to eradicate vulnerability, the need to accept failure, to open to the 'spark of the divine fire' within and to radiate that in the world. Learning to attend to the quiet impulses towards wholeness at the root of even fractured human desire; through Eckhart's teaching on letting go and letting be, or Buber's understanding of the interplay of distance and closeness in right relationship, and Graf Durkheim's way of initiatory therapy, meditation, and embodiment, I found Eckhart House a place of wisdom and encouragement. I explored further the complex and subtle dialectic between transcendent and immanent aspects of faith and theology. So too, through practising as a psychotherapist and directing courses with colleagues in Dublin and Belfast, new ways opened up in which people could discover vital connection between the call to inwardness and outwardness, vision and praxis, the mystical and the prophetic, through a stance of acceptance which reflects the mystery of hope at the core of creation.

Elected to a governance role in my congregation, I was assigned the portfolio ecumenism and peace. If I were to give leadership on this, I knew that it could only be from a methodology that brought theological theology and practice together. And so I went to study at the Irish School of Ecumenics and thence to Trinity College (innocent of the fact that after completing Masters and doctoral programmes, and after a further year coordinating the work of the Opsahl Commission in Belfast,[8] I would find myself Director of the Irish School of Ecumenics). There had been a fallow period in my theological journey and my mind was ripe for in-depth systematic study. I came with lived questions and was more aware of the need for mutually critical engagement between theology, history and the social sciences, and of the potential of theology done with eyes open to contextual and historical challenges. I continued to be interested in the impact upon scripture, theology and ecclesiology of the intervening decades of feminist, liberation and ecumenical theology and hermeneutics. New interpretative keys and practical fieldwork in other churches provided new angles of understanding on Calvin, Luther, Augustine and the great theologians of the East, and broadened the ecumenical vista. Exposure to the worlds of Judaism, Buddhism, Islam released unthought – of religious, ethical and political questions, many of them painful and unresolved. Scripture, tradition and context were all there, but presented through different intra- and inter-perspectives, calling for rigorous attention and imaginative modes of inquiry that can transcend the pre-determining limits of confessionalism. In confronting or negotiating of different publics of theology – Church, Academy and Society – I continued to recognise myself as at home in none of these three separately, but in all of them in relationship; and that is where I see the future of theology – in dialogue across churches, cultures, disciplines and traditions.[9]

As a member of our Dominican Council General, and also in collaborative work with the World Council of Churches, I found my theology informed and questioned by visits to places such as Brazil, Argentina and Southern Africa where I saw the option for the poor and the Church of the Poor as a lived reality. Among so many afflicted people whose ways of life had been devastated by injustice, violence, AIDS or devastation of ecosystems, I was constantly inspired by their capacity for solidarity and hope. The theology of hope or ecumenical solidarity – expressed in worship, protest, social analysis or human rights advocacy – came alive in township and *campo*, in Bible study with Basic Christian Communities in Buenos Aires and Rio, in three-hour liturgies in a mud church in Nyanga or in an ecumenical service in Cape Town in defiance of the

Group Areas Act. Such experiences gave blood and sinews to my ecumenical theology of justice, peace and the integrity of creation, and clearer eyes for recognising the scope of interfaith friendship, or cooperation with other people of good will.

In Ireland, increasing ecumenical involvement sharpened my realisation of the churches' comparative slowness to engage the ecumenical agenda. Often blind to our own sectarian constructions, we have been cautious in relativising our cultural identities for the sake of transcending shared gospel of peace. Standing alongside others amid the rubble of the Shankill bomb, the burnt-out Springfield Methodist Church or the devastation of Omagh has brought a different depth to my conviction about the urgency of witnessing together to our hope in Christ's resurrection. Meeting those who planted bombs and those bereaved by bombs has qualified my approach to the theology of forgiveness but convinced me even more of its necessity. All this lends an impatient edge to my ecumenical ecclesiology. Divided churches too cost lives. Prominent church leaders have demonstrated mutual support and friendship; there has been some inter-church cooperation – in youth and peace initiatives. A plethora of informal Christian initiatives also exists, in which people are working for reconciliation locally and in the wider civic sphere. The Irish School of Ecumenics (not without some church support, it should be said) has discovered among an increasing number of layfolk a desire for ecumenical learning and cooperation in building a shared future. But, churches as churches are hesitant. There is little to suggest that the ecumenical vocation belongs at the heart of the churches' self-understanding.

Ecumenical theology and practice have proved life-changing, drawing me into a journey, blessed by new friends and different sites of theological reflection. Through its lifeworld, I have come to understand my Roman Catholic belonging in a way that makes me feel both richer and more meek, through this daily economy of inter-theological study and exchange with those who are both 'other' and yet profoundly related in nature and grace. Much of my thinking has been honed to the concerns of interchurch and interfaith relationships, the interplay of religion and identity in the context of late modernity and the theology of justice and dialogue in intercultural contexts. Also, the interdisciplinary field of 'ecumenics', as epistemologically construed in ISE, has directed my theological focus into such spheres of discourse as international relations, cultural studies or social theory in ways that I continue to find fruitful for Christian theological understanding whether in respect of religious conflicts, post-Westphalia; postmodern challenges to ecumenism *vis à vis* any unexamined coercive presumptions in its own grand narrative; or the churches' failure to pursue together as churches a theology of life in protest against poor nations so scandalously crippled by debt.[10]

I am a contributor and catalyst rather than innovator, convinced of the variety of ministries in the Lord's vineyard – ploughing, planting, watering – yet knowing we must entrust the harvest to the mysterious workings of grace. The Holy Spirit may, as is her wont, surprise us, or invite us to risk the scarcities we cling to for the sake of abundant life. Varied experiences in leadership have taught me to welcome light from any quarter (for truth springs up in unexpected places) and to pray for courage when it is time to stand alone. One inestimable gift has been to witness the generosity and courage of spirit in the lives of my sisters in the Dominican Order whose fidelity and hope are a sign of Christ's incarnate love and a clue as to why love is the testifying mark of his followers. Together with my parents, family, friends and strangers living and dead, they are an icon of the Communion of Saints. We all belong together in our differences in the living stream of tradition. This thought brings me back to my starting point. So it is fitting perhaps to sum up with some brief reflections on how I now think of the relationship of faith and theology as first and second order realities in my life.

A red thread has been the grounding of critical theology in a communally shared religious spirit and through openness to meet across boundaries of tradition and culture. Newman has been a mainstay in clarifying those vexed relationships. In his schema, religion denotes the primary experience of the sacred – personal, collective and institutional – appealing to inner experience and outward commitment. Theology involves a critical and self-critical reflection on religious experience. Around either pole we wrestle, caught between the invitation to live in the light of a mystery that claims us and the contingency of our humanness. Newman testifies to the significance of living into that tension without sacrificing either claim. His clarification of different ways of apprehending God through real and notional assent – linked to an analogous correspondence between religion and theology – illuminate the roles of faith and reason in spiritual life and theological quest. I have not been willing to stay camped too long on either side of the river.[11] At the centre of this endeavour is the quest for God – the One, utterly Other, yet manifesting in us that *unknowable and knowing relationship* where there is always space for 'other' others, through faith, hope and love.

I also recall George Tyrell's reminder that we are not saved through theology, but through faith: 'Devotion and religion existed before theology, in the way that art existed before art-criticism; reasoning before logic; speech before grammar'. Therefore, when theology begins to contradict the facts of 'the life of faith and charity as actually lived', Tyrell insists, 'it loses its reality and authority and needs to be corrected by the *lex orandi*'.[12] Ironic perhaps that the insight of a condemned theologian resonates with that of the 'Angelic Doctor' who, near the end of his life, disparaged all he had written as 'so much straw – *faena, faena*' – compared to the beatific vision of the One about whom he had written. The same echo reverberates in Orthodox theology: 'All theology aspires to doxology'. And yet ... The dialectic is never resolved. It is important to acknowledge this in face of those who would make of mystery the basis for religious authoritarianism. Unsurprisingly, Tyrell also has something to say about the necessary, corrective function of critical theology.

R.S. Thomas catches the vying demands of heart and mind in a paradox: his heart says it is better to wait for God 'on some peninsula of the spirit'; his mind is 'sceptical' of such anthropomorphic fancy:

> A promontory is a bare
> place. No god leans down
> out of the air to take the hand
> ... so in everyday life
> it is the plain facts and natural happenings
> that conceal God and reveal him to us
> little by little under the mind's tooling.[13]

A self-reflection of this kind is not a CV. I have not attempted to give a thematic account of my own areas of research – for example on an ecological creation theology, cultural influences on ecumenical ecclesiology or a theology of peace in the Irish context. I have left it to other contributors to underline the importance of feminist theology or the need to find some resolution of the unsettled relationship between theology and the university in Ireland, while avowing that such realities concern me. Such is one benefit of a *community* of interpreters rich in diversity of insight, which this volume exemplifies. Not everything can be said. I have aimed to suggest that my theological journey (adapting Heaney) has taken me into 'the wideness of the world [which] became a journey into the wideness of language ... where each point of arrival ... turned out to be a stepping stone rather than a destination'.[14] Like Heaney, I never quite climbed down from the arm of that sofa.

Notes

1. Seamus Heaney, *Crediting Poetry: The Nobel Lecture* (Oldcastle: Gallery Books, 1995) 1-3.

2. Iris Murdoch, from a Platonic perspective, makes an analogous point on the inescapability for theology, of religious faith. She challenges the reasoned dismissal (à la Schopenhauer or Kant, for example) of Anselm's, 'I do not seek to understand that I may believe, but I believe in order to understand.' This is 'not just an apologist's paradox, but an idea with which we are familiar in personal relationships, in art, in theoretical studies ... [whereby] I intuitively know and grasp more than I can yet explain.' *Idem, Metaphysics as a Guide to Morals* (London: Chatto and Windus, 1992) 391-405, at 393.

3. Clifford Geertz, *The Interpretation of Cultures* (New York: Basic Books, 1973). Geertz defines culture as 'an historically transmitted pattern of meanings embodied in symbols, a system of inherited conceptions ... by means of which men [sic] communicate, perpetuate and develop their knowledge about and attitudes towards life' (p. 89). See also, Michael Walzer, *Thick and Thin: Moral Argument at Home and Abroad* (Indiana: Notre Dame Press, 1994).

4. Paul Ricoeur, *Critique and Conviction* (New York: Columbia University Press, 1998). In this extended interview the author acknowledges the coexistence of both his languages – of 'philosophical argumentation, in the public space of discussion and the profound motivation of my philosophical engagement and of my personal and communitary existence.' He avers, 'My two allegiances always escape me, even if at times they nod to one another' (p. 150). He further theorises McIntyre's idea of 'the narrative unity of a life', correlating narrative meaning to categories of memory, truth, identity and trust. Cf, ibid., *Time and Narrative*, vol. 3, trans. Kathleen Blamey and David Pellauer, (Chicago: University of Chicago Press, 1988), 157-59 and 162-164. See also, Ricoeur, *Oneself as Another*, trans. Kathleen Blamey (Chicago and London: University of Chicago Press, 1992) 121-39 and 157-68.

5. Rowan Williams put it well: 'The neighbour is our life; to bring connectedness with God to the neighbour is bound up with our own connection with God ... We love with God when and only when we are the conduit for God's reconciling presence with the person next to us.' *Silence and Honey Cakes: The Wisdom of the Desert* (Oxford: Lion Publishing, 2003) 40.

6. Ricoeur is apropos again to this juncture in my own life. Speaking of

the relationship between philosophy and religion, he points to Moses' experience in Ex 3:14 where 'the narrative context of the vocation story is torn by a kind of speculative irruption', yoking together the contrasting language of philosophy (thinking) with the biblical language of knowing *Critique and Conviction*, op. cit., 149.

7. In its emphasis, for example, on mediation through theology finding fruitful dialogue partners in philosophy of religion, Jewish thinking, depth psychology, or the new science, I felt an intellectual attraction, and a sense of the interrelatedness of Aquinas' metaphysical account of the human person's connatural relationship with Divine Being. See Paul Tillich, *Theology of Culture* (Oxford: Oxford University Press, 1959). This seemed to me aligned to Aquinas's metaphysical account of the person's connatural relationship with Divine Being or of the analogical relationship of divine being and human existence. Later I would seek out and discover studies that examined this Tillich-Aquinas relationship more explicitly. See Tillich's chapter on Aquinas in, *History of Christian Thought* (New York: Touchstone/Simon & Schuster, 1967). See also *Paul Tillich in Catholic Thought*, (ed.) Thomas A. O'Meara, OP, and Celestin D. Weisser (London: Longman & Todd, 1964), which draws out common insights between Aquinas' *analogia entis* and Tillich's on the mediating power of the symbol in the life of faith and revelation.

8. Andy Pollak (ed.), *A Citizens' Inquiry: The Opsahl Report on Northern Ireland* (Dublin: Lilliput Press, 1993).

9. See, for example, David Tracy, *The Analogical Imagination* (London: SCM, 1981) 6-31.

10. *Mutatis mutandis*, theology in an ecumenical voice has much to contribute to such discourse, informed by the gospel vision of a more just, inclusive and sustainable world, confident in its own religious and scientific grounding and its own mystical or prophetic resources, and characterised by intellectual rigour, respect for others' dignity and freedom, and willing to cooperate with others in the search for truth and peace.

11. John Henry Newman, *An Essay in Aid of a Grammar of Assent* (Oxford: Oxford University Press, 1985) 34-35.

12. George Tyrell, 'Lex Orandi, Lex Credendi', *Through Scylla and Charybdis – or the Old Theology and the New* (London: Longmans, Green & Co., 1907) 85-105. 'If any theology of grace or predestination or of the sacraments would make men pray less, or watch less, or struggle less, then we may be perfectly sure that such

theology is wrong' (104-105, and *passim*). I am indebted to my *Doctorvater*, Gabriel Daly, for helpful illuminations of Tyrell's thought.

13. R.S. Thomas, 'Emerging'. This is one of a long series of poems in which Thomas wrestles with God's absence and presence and with the human capacity by turns to know God or to live within the shadows of mystery. R.S. Thomas, *Collected Poems 1945-1990* (London: Dent, 1993) 355.

14. Seamus Heaney, *Crediting Poetry*, 11.

14.

My Journey into Theology: The Cross-Cultural Impact

Elochukwu E. Uzukwu

Initial Impulse – Twilight

I look back at a non-deliberately chosen vocation to theology that appears to focalise around encounter between gospel and culture. Will my narrative be any use to non-Africans? Africa constitutes my specific continent of interest. My areas of research and publication incline towards liturgy, sacraments and culture, and the kind of church desirable in the African context. Sometimes I blame the orientation toward liturgy and sacraments on difficulties I had early in my formative years over the 'real presence' of the Lord in the Eucharist. However, my passion for gospel and culture lies elsewhere.

Firstly, my rural upbringing possibly played a role in later interest in gospel and culture. I still prefer vacation in my village rather than in the noisy towns and cities. Secondly, I missed out on 'boys' initiation' of my age group at age five or six. I found the exclusion frustrating; the sense of loss may have contributed to my idealising cultural issues. I never blamed my father or grandfather for being Christian. I never had regrets being Christian. But life in my village in the late 1940s and early 1950s as a non-initiate was a sacrifice hard to understand. The initiated were superior to the non-initiate. My younger brother and I were inferior people. Enrolment in the primary school was sweet comfort; boys' initiation gradually fell out of use within my village-group.

The *wakeup call* to engage Christianity and culture came early during my theological education and the first years in pastoral ministry. During the Nigeria-Biafra war (the civil war ravaged Nigeria, 1967–1970) there was widespread distress. Students and staff in our theological seminary took great interest in rites of affliction (healing rites) practised in popular healing homes. The most popular in the Biafran enclave was under the supervision of Nwanyi Ufuma 'Woman of Ufuma'.[1] The rituals were a combination of traditional Igbo healing and deliverance rites with Christian Scriptures and prayers. Students submitted reports on their investigation and lively debates followed papers that were read at meetings of the students' 'Theological Circle'. We were challenged to conduct similar fieldwork into aspects of culture in dialogue with Christian practice, with no training in cultural anthropology. A colleague and I investigated divination and ritual covenanting. Our report presented in 1971 (after the civil war) was greeted with scepticism. We appeared too Cartesian in approaching the slippery craft of divination. The experience, however, kept me pondering over possibilities of fruitful contact between gospel and culture.

The *first turning point* happened during my first year in pastoral ministry. I had to face the challenge of Igbo traditional marriage and Christian marriage. Young men, of my age group, were living with their wives, but not properly or Christianly married. I put it to them during our numerous conversations that they were living in concubinage (according to my theological and canonical textbooks). Unimpressed with my rhetoric, they made me understand in no uncertain terms that were it not for the mother-in-law they would never dream of the second ritual of church marriage. They are legitimately married. (Wives supported and sustained the pressure on their husbands to undergo church marriage, for in the absence of this ritual they are deprived of the rights and privileges of belonging to the very powerful Catholic women organisation.) I took this problem to my moral theology professor and received the shocking answer:

'We discussed those issues years ago; one cannot change the canonical prescription.' That answer lowered my esteem for moral theology – a discipline so embedded in culture and yet closed to African cultural development. Our Christian communities would continue to live with parallel codes and multiple rituals (in a type of collective social schizophrenia). Yet my hunch then was that issues around marriage constituted fertile ground for encounter between gospel and our Nigerian cultures. It is instructive that time has proved the 'young rebels' right. Today, three dioceses in Nigeria (Lokoja, Ekiti and Enugu) have rules in place to celebrate Catholic marriage in the home of the bride, merging the traditional and Christian rites.

That early pastoral experience set me against any specialisation in moral theology. I directed my energy into pastoral liturgy – celebration of sacraments, especially vernacular Eucharistic celebrations that were very lively and loved by parishioners. And with a parish and a minor seminary totally under my supervision for two years, we plunged into liturgical animation with passion. For my postgraduate studies in Toronto, though I registered in the Systematic Theology department, my focus was on the sacraments and liturgy.

Toronto School of Theology was my next turning point. I was interested in historical theology (like Chalcedonian Christology, theology of the Eucharistic prayers). Furthermore, one of my mentors (Tibor Horvath) presented me with a happy challenge by advertising a course on 'Theology of Sacrifice and African Theology'. I believe he advertised the course to cater for my orientation and interest. I signed up for it and ended up doing it as a reading course, as I was the only student interested. It was a liminal experience; an initiation into African languages and cultures, history, anthropology, sociology, religions, rituals etc. I had only a nodding acquaintance with these in my early formative years. From the intensive reading course I started to develop a socio-historical approach/methodology to theological research and to discard the essentialist perception of culture for explorations in African theology.

When I applied for the doctorate, I was confronted with departmental conditions that went against my gospel and culture focus. The systematic theology department appreciated my earlier work on memory and tradition in Jewish-Christianity and the Igbo of Nigeria (M.Th. thesis). But it did not support my interest in developing a Eucharistic prayer that is Igbo and Christian, drawing from the Jewish tradition, Patristic and historical euchology and Igbo prayer traditions. I was required to specialise in a particular theologian – Tillich or Rahner or Aquinas. I had done a major seminar paper on Tillich's Christology, but I was not inclined to be a clone of Tillich, Rahner or Aquinas. My interest was to probe the Jewish-Christian tradition, explore developments in defined areas of Patristics, especially the eucharistia, and probe in detail the Igbo euchological tradition in order to create an Igbo Christian Eucharistic prayer.

I was lucky I had sympathetic advisors and mentors – especially two Hungarian Jesuits, Tibor Horvath and Attila Mikloshàzy. I changed to the department of Pastoral, Liturgy, Spirituality and Proclamation. Without abandoning the orientation in sacramentology I was obliged to take courses in spirituality, Calvinist and other Protestant liturgies and Evangelical exegesis and proclamation. I took an additional reading course with Horvath on African theology to research the methodology for probing the relationship between Christianity and African and other world religions. I was doing what I wanted and liked. Before I presented my thesis proposal I submitted for publication articles on 'Methodology for African Theology', and an assessment of 'Christian Missions' in the African continent, charting my own path towards local theology. Soon after defending my thesis on 'Blessing and Thanksgiving among the Igbo –

Towards a Eucharistia Africana', I was on my first teaching assignment to Congo Brazzaville.

Four Defining Years in the Congo

The Congo helped to define my interests and orientate research projects. Teaching in French involved doing theology almost all over again. Congo Kinshasa partly determined my research orientation. The Episcopal conference of the then Zaire had to answer queries over the evolving 'Zairian rite' between 1979 and 1982. Some of the queries from the Congregation for Divine Worship and the Discipline of the Sacraments came to my desk. The effort I made to offer clarifications made me appreciate how little known in the African church were the Christian liturgical traditions – eastern and western. It helped me to produce my first monograph – *Liturgy: Truly Christian, Truly African*.[2]

Questions by colleagues and students on gestures, rites, signs and symbols were challenging. How does one en-flesh in our context liturgies that speak, where 'the *sanctification* of the man is signified by *signs perceptible to the senses*, and is effected in a way which corresponds with each of these signs'?[3] For some time I toyed with the idea of investigating the history and archaeology of Eucharistic elements and their relevance for Africa. I published a paper 'Food and Drink in Africa, and the Christian Eucharist'[4] in which I proposed local food and drink like millet and palm wine as elements. The paper attracted attention, though I lost steam in such pursuits. I did not see much hope in their practical application. I concentrated rather on history of gestures, rituals, myths, in eastern and western Christianity and the impact those from Africa would have across the board on liturgical inculturation that respects and challenges history and context. I was not to finalise research into these before returning to Nigeria in 1982. I still kept contact with the Congo through visiting lectureship, conferences and especially the meetings of the Ecumenical Association of African Theologians.

Nigeria: A Totally Different Challenge

I was teaching in the largest seminary in Nigeria, Bigard Memorial Seminary Enugu. The orientation of most colleagues was scholastic. Ages could have separated the Bigard and Eastern Nigeria from the energy, creativity, dynamism and courage to innovate that characterised the Zairian institutes and Episcopal conference. The first probing for a change of vision was through a proposal of missiological courses in the curriculum that should include: encounter between Gospel and African cultures, facing issues of poverty, development and liberation, and interreligious dialogue. Working quietly with the dean, the proposal was finally accepted and I carried the burden of teaching the courses. It was during this time that I researched and published material on evangelisation, church and development. But it was also a period when I was less and less satisfied with the formation of laity, clergy and religious, within the limits of the structures of the church in my country, characterised by the pyramidal structures dominating the Roman Catholic Church.

The Spiritan leadership (at the generalate level and in Nigeria) and confrères, young and old, were dissatisfied with formation that did not equip one to confidently minister or serve in transcultural situations. It was time to move on and found the Spiritan International School of Theology (SIST) Attakwu – just ten kilometres away from Bigard Seminary. Our hopes were not deceived. Our programme was open to missiology, interested in cultural diversity and contextual questions, while catering for the demands of traditional Catholic theological education. In addition we planned missiological colloquiums on an annual basis. The first colloquium held in 1989 was on *Healing and Exorcism: The Nigerian Experience*. And in 1996 we held an intercontinental congress on *Africa – Towards Priorities of Mission*. The results were published and reached a wide audience.

The mission focus of SIST did not stop my research in liturgy. I wanted to put down in orderly fashion a way of studying liturgy in the African context drawing mainly from my lecture notes. The anthropology, rationality and symbolism of gestures and their ethnic base; rituals, myth-narratives and their overall transforming potential for a celebrating community, preoccupied me. In 1991 I took a sabbatical leave to write the book *Worship as Body Language – Introduction to Christian Worship. An African Orientation,* later published by Liturgical Press in 1997. The concluding chapter of the book describes and critically assesses emerging liturgical practices in various parts of sub-Saharan Africa. Reflecting today on what I considered in the book the most frequently practiced emergent Christian ritual among the Igbo of Nigeria, I find it interesting that ritual covenanting adopted from Igbo ethnic experience is dominant. Curiously this was the first feature of culture that a colleague and I researched as students of theology.

Rwandan Genocide and the Irony of Church as Family of God

During the 1991 sabbatical leave I benefited from conversations with colleagues in Paris and Toronto. One of the fruits of the time spent in Paris was being employed three years later to teach African theology at the Institut Catholique. That was 1994, the year of the African synod and the year of the Rwandan holocaust. The genocide challenged my teaching, dominated discussions and led to soul-searching over African cultures and the prophetic role of the Christian church in Africa; a church that the synod described as Family of God. The focus of discussions was not simply on who was to blame for the genocide, but more particularly: what life-enhancing structures or patterns of social organisation in Africa are retrievable to generate another type of society and church? During some post-synodal conferences in which I participated in France and Germany to address issues emerging from the African synod, I focused on renewing ecclesiological patterns. The history of African societies reveals two broad patterns of social organisation in place thousands of years before the fateful contact with modern Europe – dispersal of authority and concentration of authority in the hands of kings or queens. Whichever pattern existed, the societies inspired by African cultural experience (not under the tutelage of Arab Moslem culture) were either republican or oligarchic. They are characterised by wide-ranging consultation and deliberation, wide-ranging involvement of the people directly or through their representatives in governance. Could the resilient dynamics of such social organisation not be retrieved to influence the concept of Church as People of God and Family of God? Could these not be retrieved to challenge the tyrannies that engulfed Africa between the fifteenth and twentieth centuries? Could they not be retrieved to challenge the biases about African cultures? The post-synodal conferences and lectures enabled me to try out ideas and receive feedback. Later I gathered the fruits of these lectures and conferences in the monograph, *A Listening Church: Autonomy and Communion in African Churches,* published by Orbis Press in 1996. The book has had more impact than I anticipated, possibly because the alternative patterns of organising society I suggested survive more or less across Africa. It is not tolerated by modern African dictators by a highly centralised Roman Catholic Church dominated by monarchical episcopacy where the bishop, like the pope, has absolute power. A number of doctoral candidates have found those ideas useful in articulating their dissertation.

In Search of Renewal of Christian Theology in Africa

Since the publication of the two books I have been wondering or reflecting over methodology. Most African theologians have undergone the tutelage of the western academy and generally followed the method deeply influenced by the rationalism of the Enlightenment. I have shown independence in staying focused on issues of Gospel and culture. Yet I more or less apply the rhetoric available to those interested in Gospel and cultures – dialogue, correlation, dynamic equivalence and so on. In accounting for the African reality I settle for a socio-historical method – i.e. accounting for the social realities of African societies in their historical setting rather than describing peoples that make up our societies in essentialist immobile or changeless concepts. This in a way adapts historical criticism. While not abandoning the advantages of this method, I have come to cast doubt more and more on everything I read, on everything I write. I engage my tradition with greater confidence; appreciate positively the pessimism that inspired colonial and postcolonial African literature, and draw inspiration from the humanism that is deeply rooted in the African life-project. The common West African wisdom tradition that celebrates multiplicity or duality of every aspect of life is beginning to influence my approach to Gospel and culture. It allows greater freedom to critique my African heritage and put in inverted commas my fascination with Christian western and eastern local theologies.

I feel the need to align theological studies with the humanism that dominates African literature – drawing from the same wells, from the same cultural matrix. I am inclined to adopt the style of Chinua Achebe in embracing the overriding duality that must interlace all things: nothing stands alone, something stands and another comes to stand beside it. As Achebe reasons, in view of the little room left for the Black person in the modern world, there should neither be over-excitement nor total pessimism with regard to inherited traditions[5] – African, western Christian or any other. African scholarship must always exercise the freedom of casting a second glance at all things. In theology this freedom is comparable to the exercise of Fathers such as Clement of Alexandria, Origen and Augustine who reinterpreted, adapted and adopted the 'paganisms' of their day into Christianity – from the ritual panoply of mystery cults to the philosophical and ethical traditions.

Most African theologians – starting from the publication of *Des Prêtres Noirs s'Interrogent* in 1956[6] – depended on Western methodological tools to embed their discourse on the encounter between Gospel, culture and religion. Pioneers depended on the scholastic method while others today follow the philosophy of language. We have not boldly looked inwards for methodological tools as much as we have gone elsewhere in search of enabling systems to account for our life and history. Interdisciplinary conversation with postcolonial African literature learns from the humanistic properties that remain undying. West Africans learn from the duality or multiplicity of all things. The Igbo wisdom aphorism states, '*ife kwulu, ife akwudebe ya*' ('whenever something stands, something else will stand beside it') This essential duality of all things is a standpoint to always search for a 'second point of view', 'looking at everything twice'. This methodological standpoint influences explorations in Gospel and culture and enables the theologian to learn from bold adaptations and practices of groups like African Initiated Churches. I explored the implications of this in my contribution to *Melanges Joseph Doré* – '*L'enseignement Théologique et l'Inculturation*'.[7] Inculturation theology that subjects the whole tradition to fresh scrutiny (Vatican II, *Ad Gentes*, 22) casts doubt on patterns of orthodoxy that allow little room for difference. It enables contextual questions that challenge the Gospel and culture within specific socio-cultural milieu. Presently, I am exploring aspects of this in an uncompleted monograph – *Tradition Retrieval and Christianity in West Africa: Explorations in Inculturation*.

Notes

1. Ufuma is a village-group in South Eastern Nigeria, located south of the present Anambra State of Nigeria.
2. Elochukwu E. Uzukwu, *Liturgy: Truly Christian, Truly African*, Spearhead 74 (Eldoret, Kenya: Gaba Publications AMECEA Pastoral Institute, 1982).
3. Vatican II, *Sacrosanctum Concilium*, art. 7.
4. Elochukwu E. Uzukwu, 'Food and Drink in Africa and the Christian Eucharist' *African Ecclesial Review* XXII (1980) 370-85, 398.
5. Chinua Achebe, *Morning yet on Creation Day: Essays, Studies in African Literature* (London: Heinemann Educational, 1975); see also his *Hopes and Impediments: Selected Essays, 1965-1987* (London: Heinemann Educational, 1988); Simon Gikandi, *Reading Chinua Achebe–Language & Ideology in Fiction, Studies in African Literature Series* (Oxford: James Currey/Portsmouth, N.H.: Heinemann, 1991).
6. *Des Prêtres Noirs s'Interrogent* (Paris: Cerf, 1956).
7. 'L'inculturation et l'Enseignement de la Théologie – un point de vue africain,' in *La Responsabilité des Théologiens – Mélanges offerts à Joseph Doré*, édité par François Bousquet, Henri-Jérome Gagey, Geneviève Médevielle et Jean-Louis Souletie, Institut Catholique de Paris (Paris: Desclée, 2002) 265-272. An expanded version was published as 'Inculturation and Theological Education in Africa: Explorations in Sacramentology' *Bulletin of Ecumenical Theology* 13 (2001) 18-40.

Further Reading on Theology and (Auto)Biography

Augustine, *Confessions*, trans. and introd. E.M. Blaikock, (London: Hodder and Stoughton, 1983)

Eberhard Bethge, *Dietrich Bonhoeffer* (London: Collins, 1970)

Eberhard Busch, *Karl Barth, His Life from Letters and Autobiographical Texts*, trans. John Bowden (London: SCM, 1976)

Hans Küng, *My Struggle for Freedom: Memoirs*, trans. John Bowden (Grand Rapids/Cambridge UK: Eerdmans, 2003)

Darren C. Marks (ed.), *Shaping a Theological Mind* (Aldershot: Ashgate, 2002)

Jürgen Moltmann (ed.), *How I Have Changed* (London: SCM, 1997)

Elisabeth Moltmann-Wendel, *Autobiography* (London: SCM, 1997)

Thomas F. O'Meara, OP, *A Theologian's Journey* (New York/Mahwah, NJ: Paulist Press, 2002)

Herbert Vorgrimler, *Karl Rahner, His Life, Thought and Work*, trans. Edward Quinn (London: Burns and Oates, 1965)

Michael Walsh (ed.), *Dictionary of Christian Biography*, (London/New York: Continuum, 2001)